K.C.
IRVING

K.C. IRVING

THE ART OF THE INDUSTRIALIST

RUSSELL HUNT and
ROBERT CAMPBELL

McClelland & Stewart Limited

© 1973 by Russell Hunt and Robert Campbell

0-7710-4287-6

The Canadian Publishers
McClelland and Stewart Limited
25 Hollinger Road, Toronto

Printed and bound in Canada

CONTENTS

PREFACE

"The poet's pen
Turns them to shapes, and gives to airy nothing
A local habitation and a name."

– A Midsummer Night's Dream

This is not a book about an airy nothing. Unlike the poet's subject, ours already has a local habitation and a name. The local habitation is New Brunswick (by most methods of measuring, the poorest province in Canada) and the name is Irving (by most methods of measuring, one of the richest names in Canada). If that is a fundamental difference, however, between art and journalism – that the journalist has his local habitation and name given to him – there is also a fundamental similarity between art and the sort of journalism represented by this book. Our subject, like the poet's, has a significance and importance which transcend its context. The phenomenon represented by the Irving empire is important far beyond the borders of New Brunswick, and significant for people who have no economic connections whatever with it.

Irving is, of course, important to New Brunswick. Indeed, it's clear that had Kenneth Colin Irving not been born in Bouctouche, New Brunswick, in 1899, the province would be a startlingly different sort of place today. But that's not the reason this book exists. If the book leads to a better understanding among New Brunswickers of how their province came to be the way it is, fine; but the justification for the book's existence is wider than the scope of Irving's direct economic influence. Though the book would never have come into being had Irving *not* been important to New Brunswick, that importance itself can hardly justify such a study. What would justify it would be a significant contribution to our understanding of the way corporate enterprise works, of the methods by which it attains power and of its motives for doing so, and of the sorts of relationships that exist between such corporate structures and our society as a whole, whether in New Brunswick or Toronto or Inuvik.

For such purposes, New Brunswick's relationship with the Irving dinosaur comes as close to a laboratory situation as you're likely to find. A small society, isolated from and exploited by the larger world, and a one-man empire: in such a situation you can see the basic outlines of the relationships much more clearly than you can, say, in the relationship between Canada and the barons of the C.P.R. or between the U.S. and the oil interests.

To accomplish his understanding of similarly complex problems the social scientist generalizes. He produces, out of his examination of particulars, abstract statements of what he believes to be universal truths. The artist, on the other hand, produces an example (gives a local habitation and a name to his airy nothing). He creates a specific case, and produces understanding not by generalizing on the basis of it but by making it ever more specific, unique, and complete, until the understanding available to the reader rivals what he could have arrived at through an experience of the phenomenon itself.

Journalism is a bastard form. For most of its existence, whenever it has become more than mere reportage, it has oscillated between seeing itself as a social science and as an art, and has chosen its methods accordingly. The method of this book is based on the assumption that the journalist has far more in common with the poet than with the sociologist. What understanding our discussion of Irving has to offer of all those sociological abstractions – the relationship of corporate enterprise and the public weal, the nature of entrepreneurial motivation – is to be gained through the understanding of one specific, unique situation at a time.

Shakespeare never said that Falstaff represented a moral position or that Macbeth was an example of the dynamics of tyranny; he simply offered us Falstaff and Macbeth in terms we could understand. Just so – and we do not propose to carry the analogy with Shakespeare one step further – we offer you Irving.

In offering that phenomenon, we are making no attempt to present a complete biography of Irving the man, nor a connected and chronological history of his empire. Rather, we present a number of characteristic incidents or aspects of the development of that empire, each presented in more detail than would be possible if they were part of a history of the whole phenomenon. We offer each just as an artist offers an incident: as interesting in itself and also as part of a general portrait of a character. That in this case it is the character of a corporation and not of a personage in literature does not change the basic method of proceeding. The more complex a corporation becomes the more it exhibits patterns of behaviour, patterns we can call "characteristics".

There is something else about the method of this book that should be made clear. The information in it has been assembled almost entirely from public sources. Suspicious of the legends which have gathered around the name "Irving" in New Brunswick, and convinced that those myths are often based on nothing more than wishful thinking, we have worked almost entirely with public records – corporate registrations, land transaction registries, government briefs and reports, court records, hearings of committees and commissions, newspaper and magazine reports. While this has meant giving up many an "Irving story", it has also meant that the understanding which is attained in each instance is solidly based on the facts of the matter.

There is another reason for using public sources, and it has to do with our notion of what the function of the journalist in society can be. One of his most important functions is to stand as an example of the fact that our universe isn't incomprehensible, that it is possible by application to come to an understanding of the most apparently complex and confusing phenomena. If the journalist restricts himself to sources equally available to everyone, he serves that function better than if he acquires privileged information, interviews important people, cites anonymous sources, and so forth. When understanding arises out of materials available to everyone, the understanding is more likely to be seen, not as an arcane process which is the special skill of a few, but as an ability which the reader himself possesses.

This is a far more crucial matter than it at first might seem. The more complex our society and the institutions that make it up become, the easier it is to confuse or fool or daunt people with sheer complication, to put the public in the position of blindly trusting those in positions of authority because the complexity of the situation is beyond the understanding of anyone outside the government – or the corporation, or the school, or whatever institution one is dealing with.

It has been pointed out fairly often by people like Saul Alinsky that middle- and upper-class people traditionally have better luck dealing with governments and businesses than lower-class people, and the reason this is so is that middle-class people believe that they can come to an understanding of the methods and principles of the institution they're dealing with, and believe therefore that they can have an effect on it. But until you believe that it is possible to understand and therefore affect such institutions, you're helpless, and this has traditionally been the plight of the very poor in our society. It's not a question of intelligence, or even of ambition, but simply of having a bit of faith that the universe you live in has some order, makes some sense. And, whether because of education or simply social tradition, this faith has normally been a characteristic of the middle and upper classes in western society. Clearly, a consequence of this observation is that if we are to construct a truly open and just society we must extend that skill or faith to an ever wider proportion of the population.

Unfortunately, as the institutions we all deal with have become more complex and impenetrable, that faith has been eroded, and we are all becoming the helpless victims of the sort of corporate complexity and bureaucratic elaboration that governments and business and educational institutions seem to specialize in. Whether consciously or not – and sometimes it's pretty hard to believe that sheer complexity has not become the conscious aim of the institution – institutions solidify their power by rendering their structures incomprehensible. When the seamen on the *Irving Ours Polaire* can't get their union certified as a bargaining agent because they can't hack their way through the corporate maze and find out who they work for, they are entrapped in the very centre of the twentieth-century dilemma. And insofar as any of us comes to accept that such situations are incomprehensible or insoluble, we are all trapped in there with them.

And the more often we smack our heads against the complexity of some institution, the more often we give up on trying to influence our kids' educations, return unsatisfactory merchandise, or make sense of our tax return, the more likely we are to curl up in that strangely comfortable position with our television set and give up on the attempt to make sense out of it all.

It is in his opposition to that tide – a tide not of ignorance or apathy, but of incomprehension – that the value of the journalist (like that of the novelist or the poet) resides. See, he says, the universe does make sense. It may not be pleasant, it may not even be bearable, and it's certainly not easy to cope with, but it does make sense. It's possible to understand and – in the case of the kinds of phenomena journalists deal with – it may even be possible to alter.

Here, then, are our raw materials for an airy nothing: a local habitation and a name.

CHAPTER ONE

Portrait of a Dinosaur

The south-east shore of Grand Lake in central New Brunswick is not exactly a tourist mecca. But there are pleasant little rocky beaches, a breeze, and very often you find wild strawberry fields on the slopes coming down to the wooded shore of the lake. Around the lake the country rolls very gently; the immediate area often floods in the spring freshet, though the farmhouses themselves are well up above the level of the lake. The beaches are marvelous places for midsummer bonfires, with marshmallows and hot dogs. Along the shore of the lake are scattered, in among the trees and on the margins of beaches, thousands of well-weathered, dry, four-foot logs anywhere from three to ten inches in diameter. But when you have a beach bonfire you don't burn those. You gather brush and driftwood that is identifiably driftwood, and not pulp logs.

A visitor is likely to ask, why not – surely the four-foot logs would make a marvelous fire. Something wrong with the wood? But anyone who's lived along the shore for a few years knows why those logs are left alone. It seems that sometime in the late forties or early fifties (the date varies with the teller) an Irving log boom on its way down Grand Lake from Chipman, headed into the St. John River toward the Irving pulp mill at the mouth of the river, broke up in a storm on the lake and the logs were scattered far and wide along the coast. A few of the local residents (many of whom cut a little pulp on the side as a way of supplementing their income) began salvaging the logs, piling them along with their own logs by the side of the road, and selling them to the Irving company. An innocuous practice, it would seem; surely no industry the size of Irving's was going to care about those logs, much less try to salvage them from the thousands of inlets, bays, stream mouths and beaches where they had lodged themselves. Not so, the story goes: K. C. Irving himself went on the radio to announce that anyone "stealing" that lumber from the shores of the lake would be prosecuted: those logs were private property.

In any place but New Brunswick, such an announcement would have caused a sardonic chuckle and the pulp cutters would have merrily cut the identifying brands off the logs and sold them. Not in New Brunswick, a province which has long been well aware of K.C. Irving's penchant for going to court over insignificant matters. Hadn't Irving taken Gordon Green and Hazen Jordan of Barker's Point (just across the river from Fredericton) to court in September of 1948 for, in the words of the indictment, "fraudulently holding, without the consent of the owner, timber that was found floating in the Nashwaak" – a matter of about fifty-four logs?

So there Irving's logs rest, twenty years later. Even yet, few people gather them for fuel. No one includes them in his corded pulp stacked along the road for pickup.

Now, it is hard to be certain that the story is true. Radio broadcasts are difficult things to verify, a quarter of a century after the fact. In a province as small as New Brunswick, legends arise quickly; everyone, it seems, has an "Irving story" and all of them could be true only if Irving were two hundred years old. Yet many of those legends suggest not only insights into Irving but, more directly, insights into New Brunswick's attitude toward the man who owns it. Whatever the truth about Irving the man, Irving's corporate identity is created at least as much by what the society around it believes as by what it is in reality. And those logs are actually still there, a fact that says more about what the name "Irving" means in New Brunswick than any dry inventory of his holdings or abstract description of his political and social power – or even a scouring of the newspapers for the miles of type in their editorial and letters columns in praise of Irving.

Every New Brunswicker knows – though he may not be aware of knowing it – that K.C. Irving is a lot more than just a man. K.C. Irving is a social phenomenon on the same level of importance as a revolution or a war. And his importance is equally difficult to measure. You can't do it, for instance, by counting up how much his companies own or how much they earn, because the figures simply aren't available: one of the carefully built-in advantages of North American corporate law is that it affords nearly impenetrable cover for corporate activity. Moreover, the question of how much the Irving companies actually own is not only probably unanswerable, but also meaningless. Irving has often claimed not to know the precise extent of his holdings, or the amount of their revenues. This has struck most journalists as disingenuous, but it probably is not: after a certain point, such figures cease to mean anything. To take an example: the refinery in Saint John is often referred to as the fifty million dollar Irving refinery. But that fifty million dollar figure surely has no meaning; the refinery is not for sale, so has no market value; though it cost somewhere in the neighbourhood of fifty million dollars to build, it could hardly be duplicated for that now, given the pace of inflation since 1960. In accountants' terms, on the other hand, it would be said to have depreciated since building. On the Saint John tax rolls, it is assessed at four million dollars. According to Irving's public statements, it has never made a profit, by which logic it should be a positive liability; on the other hand, a profit is made by the Bahamian company which sells it its crude oil at an inflated price. Perhaps the two together – the refinery and the Bahamian company – could be valued? Not likely; the Bahamian company doesn't own anything but paper – and the Bahamas don't collect corporate income taxes, so no one knows how much profit it makes except Irving – and that figure, in turn, would doubtless be all but meaningless.

Nor can the Irving power be neatly or easily measured. If there ever was a company town covering 28,000 square miles, with a population of 600,000, New Brunswick is it; and the company is K.C. Irving Limited – a company that was begun by Irving and his mother and father in 1926 as a Ford dealership, but which has grown in less than fifty years to be the single most powerful economic force in eastern Canada. It has become a commonplace of journalism to list the number of contacts a visitor to New Brunswick must have with the Irving empire, from the newspaper to the gas station, from the bus line to the hardware store, from the tankers in Courtenay Bay to the dry dock where they were built. There is hardly a pie in New Brunswick worth having a finger in, in which you won't find an Irving digit. And if, in the early seventies, under the pressure of Irving's aging and partial retirement, the empire seems to be losing a bit of its cohesiveness, its monolithic accumulation of power, it is still capable of deciding the fate of governments in New Brunswick, of determining the direction taken by society as a whole in that poor and backward province. But the social sciences haven't yet developed a yardstick for measuring that kind of power, or for distinguishing the power Irving actually exercises from the influence that is there whether he chooses to exercise his power or not.

Ultimately, however, there is one sure way to understand or communicate a concept as complex and difficult to define in abstract or numerical terms as the extent of the Irving power in New Brunswick, and that is through an accumulation of suggestive specific examples. The procedure is that of the poet or novelist rather than the social scientist, and the understanding that results is an intuitive rather than discursive one – the kind of understanding that arises out of experience with, rather than knowledge about, the Irving phenomenon.

Think, for instance, about the opening of Irving's Ocean Steel plant. Not only did the company set up a heavy industry in an area that had been zoned for light, neglect to mention to the city that it was going to block streets and create traffic obstacles, but, without notice, it sealed off a road that was the only access to a fish store – which had, for five days, to throw away a ton of lobster and salmon because nobody could get to it. Had it been anyone but Irving, the company would have been prosecuted or reprimanded; but it was Irving and the city council passed the buck – along with a motion to the effect that in the *future* any company had to warn the city of such plans "so merchants in the area can arrange their business, and fire and water departments can prepare for emergencies." That kind of incident is far more valuable in understanding Irving's power than a transcript of the clauses, in the incorporation acts of Irving companies, which allow them to expropriate land, protect them from being sued for creating a nuisance, and exempt them from various taxes and charges.

Or consider the implications of the disclosure, in a government report on social welfare released in the spring of 1971, that Irving dissuades his employees from promoting the United Fund charity drive by forbidding the payroll deduction method of donation for his more than 7,000 employees in the city. The disclosure was held for a day by Irving's newspaper until answering statements by Irving and Irving partisans could be run with the disclosure. And instead of the expectable flurry of statements deploring such antisocial and uncharitable behaviour, there was a flood of protest in the letters columns of the paper against the attack on Irving, claiming it was based on jealousy and envy. A characteristic letter said in part: "It is high time that an end was brought to these continuous attacks on Mr. Irving and his business interests by people who apparently have little or no appreciation of the amount of courage, determination, ambition and energy that he has exercised in developing industries which have played such a large part and influence on the economy of this province."

Suffice it to say, then, that Irving's power, influence and prestige in New Brunswick and eastern Canada are so immense and pervasive that they cannot adequately be described, but must be experienced in terms of specific instances. But while it may be impossible to delineate the limits of Irving's empire very clearly, there are some things that can be said about it, and that it is necessary to make clear at the outset.

It is important to bear in mind, for instance, that no organization as large and complex as the Irving dinosaur can be entirely the responsibility of one man – even when that man is Kenneth Colin Irving. "Irving" as a phenomenon – the subject of this book – is not the same thing as K.C. Irving the man. When Irving's oil dock spilled oil in the Bay of Fundy and Irving officials at first denied any knowledge of the spill – while simultaneously ordering tankers to hold out to sea while the pipeline was repaired – you can't infer that the inconsistency or dishonesty involved the personal decision of Kennth Colin Irving. When Irving's companies respond to "betrayal" with vindictive and often irrational intensity and resort to excessive use of litigation and expressions of public outrage, you can't infer that the emotions involved are those of K.C. Irving himself.

But you can say, in both cases and in many other similar ones, that the responses are typical of the kind of organization Irving has created; that in important ways it is his creation, and bears the stamp of his personality, much as the lines spoken in a play reflect the personality of the playwright even though they aren't necessarily things he would say himself. Human personality proceeds from the most complex organism known; as a corporation gets more complex, as it acquires styles and traditions of doing things – often quite unenunciated, but nonetheless discoverable principles of action – it acquires personality. And, of course, corporations are, legally, persons, some of which exhibit more personality than others.

The Irving entity is an exceptionally clear case. The corporate personality has continued to grow and develop on its own, so that the corporation often does things that its creator never would have done. In fact, one of the most common observations about the Irving empire is that its public character sometimes bears almost no relation to the private character of its creator. For instance, Senator Charles McElman remarked that the Irving empire "displays none of the gentle or considerate attributes of the man. Its thirst for power and more power is insatiable." And the late Ralph Allen wrote in *Maclean's* that Irving's "personal manners bear so little resemblance to his corporate manners that some of the people who have seen him lose his temper or heard him hurl his clipped insults toward his permanent or temporary foes have put it down to business tactics rather than blood pressure."

It is a fascinating exercise in speculation to consider the relation between the man and his creation. Testimony about the man is unanimous in describing him as a gentle, polite, gracious, and unassuming – yet as a public figure and in his businesss dealings his characteristic posture is either one of ruthless entrepreneurial aggression or of boundless moral outrage. Psychologists, no doubt, would have a lot to say about the stupendous capabilities of the human mind for constructing elaborate systems to express its inmost feelings without acknowledging them. And just as such theories are inadequate to explain poems or cathedrals, so they fail to explain K.C. Irving Limited. But in the same way that we may wish to know something of the milieu and childhood of a sculptor or poet in order, not to explain, but to understand something of his work, so it is interesting to look at the ground from which K.C. Irving sprang.

His hometown is Bouctouche, about halfway between the mouth of the Miramichi River and Moncton on New Brunswick's North Shore. Founded in 1784 by five Acadian families returning from exile, the village has always been overwhelmingly French and until the middle of the twentieth century was predominantly a fishing village, largely because of its fine harbour. When, a few score years after its founding, Herbert Irving, K.C. Irving's grandfather, arrived from Scotland, it can hardly have been an occasion recognized as one which would determine the entire future of the community. But today the visitor to Bouctouche feels the Irving presence at a saturation level. There are two gas stations on the main street – both of them Irving stations. There is one large combination department and grocery store – the Irving store. There is one large visible industry, Kent Component Homes – an Irving company and the second largest employer in Bouctouche. If you stand on the now-deserted dock where Irving's shipyards built Minca invasion barges during the second world war, the panorama doesn't include anything not owned by Irving, from the Irving station on the far left through the Irving family home across the street from the bay (and precisely in the centre of all the activity), to the Irving oil storage tanks across the water on the right. Beyond and above the panorama you can see forest, most of which belongs to the county's largest employer, J.D. Irving Woodlands.

To a casual visitor, Bouctouche seems to be doing better than the other communities in poverty-stricken Kent County; certainly there are a number of people making enough money to build new homes and paint old ones. But even as the centre of the Irving empire, Bouctouche has not escaped the trap of poverty that holds the entire North Shore: unemployment is still rife, especially among the Acadians, who form the overwhelming majority of the population. Most of what jobs there are are seasonal or occasional – Kent Homes itself, for instance, has a staff which varies from thirty to one hundred people depending on the state of the market. And of course the other main occupations, pulp cutting and fishing, are both seasonal and at the mercy of rapidly fluctuating markets. So the façade of middle-class prosperity that Bouctouche exhibits to the casual visitor is no more than a façade – a fact which a side trip down any of the back roads will verify. Though the presence of Irvings over a period of a little more than a century has made an overwhelming difference to the segment of Bouctouche that "counts", it has probably not changed the destiny of those shack-dwellers and broken farmers an iota. And in many ways the basic social structure of Bouctouche cannot have changed much since Kenneth Colin Irving was born there on March 14, 1899. At that time, as now, a small, commercially-dominant Anglophone minority ran things with a gracious *noblesse oblige,* while the majority of Acadians either remained casual labourers or moved away. Growing up in such a world must have conditioned the way little Kenneth

Colin saw himself and his relationship to other people, and it is tempting to speculate that some of his most fundamental tendencies – toward the centralization of power, toward the use of personal charity rather than institutional reorganization; toward, that is, a sophisticated form of paternalism – must have grown out of his experience of the relationship between those two cultural groups in Bouctouche in the early twentieth century.

The sources of other qualities that may have helped make Irving what he is can be guessed at in his childhood. He was brought up, for instance, in a tradition of successful Presbyterian entrepreneurship. There is a widespread myth that Irving is a self-made man, rising from clerkship in a small rural general store to his present position. Forget it. Irving's father, J.D. Irving, was one of the most powerful and wealthy men on the North Shore; for his day and location, his interests and powers were almost as extraordinary as K.C. Irving's are for his. Owner of vast tracts of Kent County, as well as land elsewhere in New Brunswick, operator of mills and stores, interested in shipping and involved in the Saint John financial scene, J.D. Irving's economic position offered a secure base from which his son could operate. Many of K.C. Irving's early undertakings, in fact, were underwritten by his father. Beyond such childhood endeavours as reclaiming binder twine and raising ducks, business enterprise takes capital as surely as it does an entrepreneurial imagination – and young Kenneth had access to both.

He had other advantages which perhaps helped him to see beyond the borders of Bouctouche and Kent County: he went to Dalhousie University and to Acadia University for short periods; to England for training as a pilot (though he never saw action); and at one point he and a friend contemplated going to Australia and actually made it as far as British Columbia before they turned back to Bouctouche. Thus when, in the early twenties, he started a gas station and Model-T dealership in connection with his father's general store, he was in a position to be able to see which way the world was going, and predict what fields might repay investment and effort. And his perception that the internal combustion engine was going to dominate the twentieth century suggests that Irving's travels had been truly educational.

But there was more than a coolly intellectual prediction of growth involved in Irving's decision about the direction his endeavours were to take. That decision was a characteristic one; it was a choice of physical objects – automobiles, gas, oil – over symbols of objects. One of the most important differences between Irving and the majority of successful entrepreneurs is that while others habitually see the world in terms of abstractions, working with paper, Irving deals in objects. In gas stations, oil storage tanks, automobiles, trees, refineries, tankers. The abstractions are there as well, of course; but first there are objects. This in part explains why Irving stayed in New Brunswick while other gigantically successful – and less successful – entrepreneurs left for the world of high finance in New York, Montreal, London or Toronto. Irving's older half-brother John Herbert Irving, for instance, went to Montreal and worked as a stock and bond broker. In such a place you could wear a white shirt and deal with abstractions with clean hands: but in New Brunswick everything had to be built before it could be bought. Even the builders' tools themselves were not yet ready to hand, but had to be forged.

That affinity with the concrete physical object was demonstrated in Irving's first business conflict, his famous dispute with Imperial Oil in 1924. Many of the other Buctouche merchants apparently objected to being forced to buy oil from their competition, so Imperial decided to take the franchise away from Irving and set up a new one. Irving's response, characteristic in several ways, was to tell Imperial where to get off; he borrowed enough money to put in his own storage tank and buy a supply of oil, and went into business himself – in competition with Imperial Oil. This was a characteristic act in that it involved, not merely paper and franchises, but a genuine, physical oil storage tank and a shipment of gasoline from Charles Noble and Company, Tulsa, Oklahoma. It was also a characteristic response in another way. Part of the motive for the audacious decision to go into competition with the giant company was moral indignation and outrage. They hadn't even bothered to inform him before cancelling his franchise.

That capacity for outrage, and that tendency to let outrage govern business decisions, was and has remained typical of the Irving corporate personality. It is easy for Irving himself to feel moral anger or outrage. His strict Presbyterian background has left him, if not holier than thou, holier than most. He neither drinks nor smokes nor swears; he fits, in fact, the archetypal pattern of the Protestant businessman. If financial success isn't a representation of grace, it will do just as well, thank you; through most of his active life, Irving may have been at St. John and St. Stephen's Church in Saint John every Sunday, but he was at work every other day. All day. The only recreation he ever seems to have allowed himself was a little fishing on the Restigouche or the Miramichi rivers (Irving companies still hold vast fishing tracts on those rivers), but in later years he seems to have given even that up. He seems either to make no distinction between work and play, or to regard what most people call play as a waste of time. The creation of his corporate empire seems to have required all the effort and creativity he could generate, and to have satisfied his competitive instincts and his desire for play as well as any man's hobbies could. All in all, at least in the early years, he came to terms with his world on a basis that was perfectly satisfactory to him, and one which allowed him to hold the typical view that the frailties of his fellow man were moral matters rather than psychological or sociological ones.

In turn, that conscious rectitude, that moral certainty, leads to an attitude toward "justice" that makes Irving one of the most litigious men in Canada. He – and his companies – are characteristically far more concerned with "justice" than with the corporate balance sheet. One of the most popular Irving stories was originally told by a barrister who had worked for him, who explained that normally a lawyer tries to keep his client out of court, but that Irving wanted to fight everything through to the finish. On one really difficult case a lawyer advised him to settle out of court. "I don't believe I asked you for a verdict," Irving said to his lawyer. "I was inquiring if you'd care to represent me." Such stories have created a reputation which has very often made it unnecessary for Irving to go to court. Nobody picks a fight with the toughest kid on the block, so it's rare to find anybody from New Brunswick fighting Irving.

His preference for dealing with objects rather than abstractions is, obviously, congruent with that tendency toward righteous anger. Were it not that he was more interested in getting satisfaction from some specific person or company than in making a paper profit, Irving would settle many cases out of court, or allow people to get away with lifting a few cords of lost pulpwood. But Irving has always felt more strongly about the specific than the general, has always had the dirtiest hands around the conference table. In the *Atlantic Advocate* for July of 1960 Russel H. Fraser, an Irving dealer in Halifax, explained how he started dealing in Irving gasoline:

"Up until 1928 I sold several other varieties of gasoline. One day, Mr. Irving came along and asked me to put in another pump to sell his gasoline. I had just finished paying for the installation of the other pumps and told him I didn't have any more money to play around with then. He told me he would help, and he really meant it, for he was soon back in overalls, ready to go to work. With a pipe-fitter to help him, Mr. Irving made the installation himself right here under the floor of the building."

There is perhaps another lesson to be drawn from Irving's challenge to Imperial Oil. It has to do with guts. It was, after all, Imperial Oil, one of the world's largest and most powerful companies, that Kenneth Colin Irving was challenging. And even if hindsight, with its realization that Irving's gas stations now vastly outnumber Esso's in the Maritimes, makes his challenge seem a reasonable one, still, from the vantage point of 1924 it certainly must have looked pretty hopeless to an outsider. And that kind of challenge, too, was to prove a hallmark of Irving's career – which includes confrontations with the Canadian National Railway (which told him, in 1937, to stop shipping his oil by boat up the St. John River; Irving not only refused, but stopped dealing with the C.N.R. altogether, building his own fleet of barges and trucks to transport his oil), the Saint John city government, the New Brunswick government, and such giant international business concerns as Sogemines, Patiño, and Standard Oil of California.

Equally important among the personality traits Irving passed on to his corporate creation is patient perseverance. As is most dramatically demonstrated in the mammoth twelve-year battle for the bus franchise in Saint John, Irving and Irving's enterprises can never be safely counted out of any fight. In fact, the longer the conflict goes on and the more interim defeats Irving suffers, the more strongly he is likely to fight – both because of his tendency to allow anger to control business decisions and because he and his organizations have always made a point of learning from defeats; learning how to use the media to their own advantage, how to employ political influence or corporate secrecy, how and where to apply economic pressure.

There are other aspects of the Irving corporate personality which are perhaps less fundamental, and probably more closely allied to business tactics than to personality. For instance, Irving's and his corporate creation's attitude toward New Brunswick and toward "foreigners", "outsiders". Irving's self-proclaimed love of his home province seemed for decades never to be out of print, whether in his own public statements or in articles about him. This begins with his very first public notoriety, in the bus franchise fight in Saint John in the thirties, during which he repeatedly insisted that his businesses had "chosen" to locate in Saint John not out of the desire for profit, but out of local patriotism. It continues through to his departure from New Brunswick and Canada on December 22, 1971. Consistently, Irving has – one hardly knows whether to say, "used this technique" or "expressed this attitude"; the two are almost indistinguishable in the man and in the company.

That it is a technique as well as an attitude there can be no doubt. His motive for using it in the first place was to gain concessions from the Saint John Common Council, both for sentimental reasons (out of fellow-feeling for another New Brunswicker and a patriotic one at that) and for solid business reasons. ("Look," he says over and over, "at how much good my presence does. Look at how many people I employ, how much capital I invest, how much economic activity I generate. And consider what my departure might mean.") The problem of the sincerity of his local patriotism is a complex one; it is so much to his advantage to seem to love New Brunswick that many people tend to assume the love is dissembled. Others, of course, do not. When Irving responded to Brigadier Michael Wardell's (then publisher of the Fredericton *Daily Gleaner* and the *Atlantic Advocate*) asking him why he stayed in New Brunswick by saying, "Because I love New Brunswick. I would not want to be anywhere else," Wardell clearly took the statement at face value, commenting only, "It is as simple as that. K.C. Irving *is* New Brunswick." To less ingenuous Irving-watchers, however, the problem is much more complex. Take, for instance, his public statements about foreign-owned oil companies.

In 1962, Irving made a public statement to the effect that foreign-dominated and Upper-Canadian oriented firms were raising the price of crude oil from Western Canada, on the pretext that the devaluation of the Canadian dollar made it necessary. "When the foreign-controlled companies are through with their battle," he said, "some of us Canadians hope we will still be here." That certainly seems a characteristic Irving utterance; not only did it play on local loyalties, but it constituted another thrust in the long-standing fencing match with Imperial Oil, who were the prime movers in the price hike. But when Imperial riposted by pointing out that Irving was unaffected by whatever might happen to Western Canadian crude because "he imports his crude through an international oil company which owns an unrevealed but substantial interest in his oil operations," a good deal of doubt was cast on the sincerity of Irving's patriotism. A good deal more arose out of the speech in the Senate a few years later by Charles McElman, who showed that Irving's international operations allowed him – like other oil companies which do not share his claims of patriotic commitment – to escape local taxation. This is part of McElman's speech in the Senate, March 10, 1971:

"The crude oil is brought by water from either the Persian Gulf or Venezuela. In the Irving case it goes physically to the Saint John refinery. But on paper it goes to that convenient tax haven, the Bahamas. Two companies become involved. For purposes of discussion we will call them Eastern Trading and Western Trading. Eastern is a Bahamian company, which buys the crude at the low source price. Eastern sells the crude to Western, the Canadian company, at a vastly inflated price.

"The price is so high that the poor refinery operation is in trouble. Some years it cannot even show a profit or pay the national wage rate to its employees. Other years it can squeeze out a small profit and pay a correspondingly small corporate tax to the Federal Government. It is really to be pitied.

"It is very interesting to note that at this very point in time this refinery, because of this arrangement, either loses money on paper or pays a very small tax. At this very moment it is in the process of almost tripling its production capacity, at the expenditure of many millions of dollars, from 50,000 barrels to 135,000 barrels per day – presumably in order to lose more money, but not for the Bahamian outfit."

It is easy to assert that such cynical manipulations prove Irving's duplicity in claiming to love New Brunswick and Canada, but the situation may well be much more complex than that. Loving a country or a region and loving its government are two quite different things, and many indubitably patriotic citizens pay tax lawyers to locate, and manoeuvre through, the chinks in the tax laws that have thoughtfully been left by the other tax lawyers who wrote them in the first place.

It is in considering such questions that the problem of the relation between Irving and his corporate creation looms largest; for while a man may be either sincere or insincere or some impossibly complicated combination of both, a corporation can only be what it does. Its beliefs only exist in its actions. In such terms, it isn't difficult to figure out whether corporations – which traditionally take advantage of such tax loopholes, which constitutionally and by nature pay as little as they can for labour and charge as much as they can for their product – love anything. In such cases protestations of patriotic motives can be nothing more than propaganda. The difficulties arise when K.C. Irving, a man in whom such emotions are almost certainly sincere, says, as a spokesman for the corporation, that its decisions are made on such a basis. And it is not simply a matter of saying that while the man may be sincere, the corporation must be judged only by its actions. Beyond a certain point, the man himself comes to be as much the corporation's creature as it is his. It may be at some such point that decisions such as Irving's leaving New Brunswick to take up residence in the West Indies in order to escape taxes are made.

In large measure, in any case, Irving's attitudes toward "outsiders" and his preference for local ownership and control of industry are certainly genuine, though complicated by self-consciousness. Irving is aware that the public expression of such opinions appeals to the Maritime knee-jerk xenophobia that he knows so well, to the side of the Maritimer's character which causes him habitually to refer to "Upper Canadians" with the kind of deprecating hostility normally reserved for the family's black-sheep cousins. Thus when, in 1970, magazine editor and university professor Donald Cameron called him to make an offer for the Fredericton *Daily Gleaner,* Irving's first question was not "how much?" but "how long have you lived in New Brunswick?" And when, in July of 1961, a spokesman for Canadian Oil claimed recklessly that his was the only Canadian-owned oil company operating in the Maritimes, there was hardly a Maritimer who didn't cheer Irving's characteristic and well-publicized statement pointing out that Irving Oil not only existed but was a good deal more important to the region than Canadian was. "Let's not forget," he concluded –

clearly playing to the gallery – "that in some cases Upper Canadians are the worst type of foreigners."

That Irving is aware of the value of such public-relations gambits as this there cannot be much doubt, though most commentators have chosen to stress his retiring nature, inferring that what Irving wants is no public image at all. Stories involving Irving's retiring and even secretive nature are legion. When, for instance, he bought the Saint John Drydock in 1959, the first newspaper to get a hint of the deal was the Halifax *Chronicle-Herald.* When they called him to confirm the story, he would say only, "You never know what might happen." And certainly there is a minimal amount of news about him in the New Brunswick papers. It was said for years that there was a standing rule at the Saint John papers that Irving's name was never to be mentioned without checking with management. However that may be, it is certainly true that there has been less media coverage of his activities than of any comparably important person. In August 1971, *Star Weekly* decided to do an article on millionaires in Canada. What they got on Irving was a seventy-word biography and a picture of his house in Saint John. And that's all. Irving clearly doesn't think his personal life is anyone else's business, and he has developed an inordinate caution about divulging his own business plans.

In spite of this, however, he is very conscious indeed of the value of a public image, and he has created a very specific kind of image for himself. From the time he first began to operate in Saint John certain aspects of his activity have in fact been fairly widely publicized: his local patriotism, for instance; his litigiousness; the vast extent of his interests (and the fact that they may be even vaster since their limits are not known); his position as an important figure behind the scenes in the provincial Liberal Party. Power is always part substance and part shadow, and beyond a certain point the shadow itself attains substance. K.C. Irving is most certainly vividly aware of this, and the creation of the shadow of power has been one of his most consistent endeavours and one of his most spectacular successes. There is no way to calculate the number of actions people have decided against because of the fear, created by that shadow as much as by real power, of Irving's reaction. In the spring of 1972, for instance, the New Brunswick government proposed taking away from certain corporations in the province the right, which some of them had enjoyed for more than twenty years, to expropriate lands to their own uses. But a number of people pointed out obliquely that Irving wasn't likely to care for that, and the project withered. Or consider the Combines Investigation of the Irving interests for operating a newspaper monopoly: the major problem faced by them, like Senator Keith Davey's Senate inquiry into the mass media, was drawing the line between actions actually willed by Irving and his interests on the one hand, and actions undertaken out of fear of Irving or anticipation of his wishes on the other.

His image is not only one of undefined power, either. One of the most important aspects of Irving's reputation is involved with the common identification of him with the province itself; in many ways he has become a symbol of New Brunswick. When Michael Wardell said "K.C. Irving *is* New Brunswick," he was not only confirming that he himself worships the man, but speaking for a sizable segment of the population of the province. When Irving marched to the Provincial Legislature in 1965 to protest aspects of the Liberal government's reformist "Equal Opportunity" program, the Saint John *Telegraph-Journal* called him "the voice of New Brunswick." And it seems clear that Irving himself sees his position in similar terms. During the Senate mass media hearings, Senator J. Harper Prowse engaged in an exchange with Irving which makes fascinating reading. Pursuing a line of questioning having to do with the way Irving's ownership of the New Brunswick newspapers related to control of the papers, Prowse asked Irving whether, if he thought an editorial policy was likely to damage the province, Irving would step in himself. Irving agreed that he would. Prowse then went on to list some of Irving's interests in New Brunswick:

"Now then, in our research, we got a lot of detail and I find that the K.C. Irving group have the major financial interest in the oil refinery, some 3,000 retail outlets for gas, oil and auto accessories; fuel oil and fuel oil retail distribution; residential propane gas distribution; shipbuilding and repair; a fleet of deep sea vessels; tug boat company; fishing vessels; a major pulp mill; saw mills; approximately two million acres of forest land, some in free hold and a little less in forest management licences, I believe; then with more in Québec and in the State of Maine; aircraft; plumbing and heating, electrical and industry supporting and building supplies and equipment, manufacturing of light and heavy industrial equipment and machinery. ... I think one of the figures that I had was that you have something like 13,000 employees that you provide work for altogether. ... So that anything that hurts New Brunswick is going to, in one way or another, hurt K.C. Irving's interests?"

"Yes," Irving replied. Then, a bit suspicious, "Would you repeat that statement?"

Prowse obliged. "Anything that would hurt New Brunswick in any way, that would depress the level of activity, confidence in New Brunswick, or hurt it in any way, would have an adverse effect on the Irving interests."

Irving was mollified. "Yes. That would be a natural assumption."

Senator Prowse sprang his trap. "And would the converse also equally be true?"

"Yes."

At that point in the hearing, by a coincidence even a third-rate novelist would never invent, the lights went out, and it took a few minutes before proceedings resumed. When lights were restored, Prowse went on to a clearer statement of the implications of his last question, almost stuttering in his eagerness to pin Irving down. "In effect, if anything hurt – it could be because you have your eggs in the one basket – if anything were to happen which was going to, or was going to appear to happen, which was going to hurt the Irving interests, this would be a threat to the New Brunswick economy and to New Brunswick?"

But having had a few moments for consideration, Irving was not going to be caught again. "I am not sure of your reasoning," he said, "I think we are kind of grasping at straws."

But everyone else was sure of Prowse's reasoning. If "K.C. Irving *is* New Brunswick", then the instincts for self-preservation and patriotism merge, because it is impossible to distinguish between the interests of K.C. Irving Limited and those of New Brunswick. "L'état, c'est moi."

A common error, and, because it is so close to being an accurate description of the situation, an understandable one. But if it is seen as one of the most fundamental considerations supporting Irving policy, it becomes much more difficult, in situations of conflict, to explain Irving's actions as mere villainy. To understand all may not necessarily be to forgive all, but it certainly renders hatred more difficult.

As any practising casuist knows, such confusion of interests renders doublethink and self-deception remarkably easy. A primitive form of this deception occurs when Irving, in apparent sincerity, claims that lavish provincial subsidation of his industries is good for New Brunswick. The argument that the generation of economic activity at whatever cost benefits the province by employing people and instituting what economists call the "multiplier effect" (an industry not only creates jobs which give people money to spend in new stores and consumer service organizations, but also generates ancillary industries because of the proximity to their source of supply or their market, which in turn generate jobs, and so forth) is a plausible one. Irving does, after all, employ almost ten per cent of the province's work force.

A more sophisticated form of this argument is employed in many cases. In the late forties, for instance, Irving discovered workers coming into the C.N.R. yards in Moncton from the Shediac shore and Memramcook regions were staying off his buses in droves and forming car pools. Characteristically, he tried to force legislation through the provincial government forbidding such car pools. Now the mental gymnastics required to conclude that *that* is good for the province are more complex, but the principle remains the same. If people are allowed to avoid riding the bus when they want to, the bus will prove uneconomical to run and will be taken off altogether, thus leaving the entire burden of transportation on the car pools – which, of course, will be significantly less reliable than the bus, running as they do on community co-operation rather than on profit. Moreover, all the people who work for the bus line – drivers, supervisors, ticket sellers, garagemen – will be thrown out of work, which will depress the local economy.

And of course in some cases the argument becomes absolutely baroque, as in the defense of Irving's newspaper monopoly before the Senate Mass Media Committee on the grounds that anything good for K.C. Irving is good for New Brunswick.

Any consideration of the sources and nature of power is incomplete without a look at the major way in which power is wielded in our society – politics. The problem posed by Irving's position in New Brunswick politics is, like so many other issues surrounding this man, almost incomprehensibly complex. He himself has repeatedly denied mixing in the political life of the province. As early as 1953 he told *Maclean's*, "I don't think politics and business mix. New Brunswick is too small for politics." A strange remark for a man who has never made any secret of his Liberal bias, a man who has never hesitated to apply the most excruciating pressure to governments to get what he wants. But it would be an oversimplification to call it a lie. What Irving means by "politics" seems to be something a lot more like direct personal involvement in the conduct of a campaign than politics in the broader political-science definition. And in such terms the statement is sincere. Irving has never involved himself openly in a political campaign – not even the highly explosive 1967 campaign in which almost every politician in the province knew that the opposition candidate had been hand-picked by Irving. For his involvement is never overt and rarely direct, and much of the power that is evident is in fact not exerted at all, but is simply the result of people being constantly aware of Irving's presence and being able to guess what his desires would be.

The extent of Irving's involvement in public affairs in New Brunswick, like so much else about him, can only be apprehended clearly through specific examples. One classic instance is the story of his relations with the government of Louis Robichaud, a story that we will discuss in detail in Chapter Four; another is the saga of his battle with the city of Saint John over the Little River water rights in the early sixties.

The story began in 1956 when Irving, using a promised multi-million dollar Kraft mill in Lancaster and a hint of a paper mill as bait, began angling for a subsidized water arrangement with the city of Lancaster (which later was amalgamated into Saint John). If, he said in April 1958, he could get a guaranteed water supply (he wanted a minimum of 23,000,000 gallons per day on a 350 day per year basis) at an acceptable price, he was prepared to go ahead with the kraft mill. The deal that was finally worked out involved a fixed annual charge of $35,000 (which was to go toward costs of construction of a new pipeline) along with drastically reduced consumption charges amounting to a cent per thousand gallons for the first nine million gallons per day, and a half-cent per thousand after that. (In contrast, the Rothesay Paper Corporation, set up a few years later, pays more than three times that; Atlantic Sugar, a long-standing Saint John industry, pays rates beginning at five cents per thousand – and the New Brunswick Electric Power Commission is socked for twelve cents. Private households and small business are in another league altogether, paying water rates on the order of twenty-five to forty cents per thousand.)

By the first of May the Act incorporating the arrangement had been passed by the Legislature. At the same session, coincidentally, another Irving Act was passed, which was to become involved with the water rates; it incorporated Irving Refining Limited, which was to operate the new refinery Irving was building at East Saint John. One of the sections of that Act also involved water: it granted Irving Refining a lease on the Little River watershed outside Saint John for one thousand dollars a year until 1990.

The deals were good ones for Irving, of course, and at first the city was pleased because they both involved significant industrial expansion. But in strictly financial terms, the cities involved had been raped. The price for the Little River lease was low, but that was not crucial; it was the arrangement for the company's participation in the pipeline construction costs which left Saint John in a disastrous financial position. By September 1959, the city was finishing the first pipeline to supply Irving's mill and the bill was already $1,063,492. The expansion of the Loch Lomond watershed system which was called for in the agreement was estimated at anywhere from three to seven million dollars, and the city simply didn't have it. Within thirteen months of the original agreement (which was signed in October 1958), the city was trying to get out of the deal. A new city government had been elected in the meantime and were in office ten months before the council got the figures on the arrangement. As soon as they did, the new mayor, David L. MacLaren, wrote the company arguing that the commitment was simply impossible for the city to manage and requesting negotiations toward modifying the arrangement. Irving's response was that the deal had been made, that Kimberly Clark was coming in on the basis of the water arrangement, and that the city had better get busy on its end of the bargain. The mill was going to need 30,000,000 gallons of water per day when completed, and the present arrangements could supply 18,000,000 at most.

By the following spring no progress had been made. Moreover, it was pretty clear that there was going to be yet another gigantic water consumer in the area, as the combine sponsoring Rothesay Paper began negotiations with the city toward a water and tax arrangement which would entail yet another mammoth expenditure. The only way out that the city could see was to go back to square one and start over, possibly using Rothesay and Irving to bid against each other. Accordingly, the city hired a lawyer and authorized him to tell Irving that the city considered the agreement "invalid" and "would take no further steps under it" – and that accounts as prepared and rendered according to what the assessment department considered a fair industrial rate (rather than the 1958 agreement rate) would have to be paid. The city said that it would absorb the entire cost of the pipeline and that it would not take steps to extend the Loch Lomond watershed, because any such extension would result in a twenty-five to thirty per cent increase in the water bills of the average citizen. The city's principal legal argument was that the council had not had the authority to fix water rates, that such matters had to be done through the assessment office – which had not been consulted, and which, in fact, had lodged a complaint about the lack of consultation the previous August.

Simultaneously, there was another development involving Irving that spring, one that no one could have suspected would turn out to be the decisive factor in the water dispute. The long-standing dream of Maritime industrial developers and politicians, the Chignecto Canal project, stirred itself again. The Chignecto Canal is one of those projects which looks marvelous on a map, but whose benefits are not nearly as clear when you're eight hundred miles away in Ottawa as they are when you're sitting on the edge of Saint John harbour and calculating sea mileages to Montreal or to northern Europe. Agitation toward getting Ottawa to build the canal had been going on desultorily since before the turn of the century; the latest flurry involved Brigadier Michael Wardell, who recently had been elected chairman of the reconstituted Chignecto Canal Committee. He got it into his head that it was the belief of "economists" connected with the federal government that if a hundred million dollars worth of new business investment in the Bay of Fundy area would be generated by the canal, it would be worth it. Accordingly, in his literal-minded way, he charged out to collect a hundred million dollars in pledges of new industrial investment contingent on the building of the canal. It wasn't long before he returned with pledges amounting to $106,806,000. As almost anyone familiar with the way things work in those circles might have predicted, exactly $100,000,000 of the total, by some coincidence, was pledged by one of the canal's longest-standing promoters and surest beneficiaries – K.C. Irving.

Wardell, with a touching faith that Irving's word would be taken as bond anywhere in the civilized world, took his piece of paper to Ottawa and, he said later, "I was told confidentially that on the strength of Mr. Irving's good name his signed pledge was to be acceptable without the detail and the canal would be built." The federal government did take the whole thing seriously enough (the premiers of both Nova Scotia and New Brunswick met with Prime Minister Diefenbaker over it) to write Irving asking him what, specifically, he was proposing. But Irving ignored one letter and replied to the other that the details of the proposal were his business. He explained later that, "When making the commitment to the Chignecto Canal Committee, it did not occur to me that I would be expected to disclose details of just what I had in mind. In the competitive atmosphere existing today, such a disclosure would be unwise and could be disastrous." If the paranoiac picture of dozens of hungry industrialists, waiting to leap at the opportunity of investing a hundred million dollars in the Bay of Fundy as soon as Irving tipped his hand, seems a little phantasmagoric, the alternate hypothesis – that Irving's "plans" were as yet nonexistent and represented pious hope as much as blueprint – had at least plausibility to recommend it to the federal government. At any rate, the government did what you would expect it to do if it didn't believe Irving, or if it took the hundred million dollar figure as what it sounded like to everybody but Wardell – cocktail-party spitballing. The government did nothing, and all the fuss about the canal was confined to central New Brunswick, where the pot continued simmering fitfully.

Another pot that was just below the boiling point all winter and the following spring was the fight over the pulp mill's water rates agreement, which reached court on May 2, 1961, when the city launched its claim against Irving for the difference between what he was paying (the agreement rates) and what the city claimed was a fair industrial rate. Over the course of the summer, the court found against the city and the city decided to appeal.

By July, however, the city government was preoccupied. The Irving Refining Company had "inadvertantly" neglected to pay its first installment on the lease on the Little River watershed. The city's suspicion – that it was hardly a mistake, but rather an attempt to introduce another issue into the fight over the pulp company's water rates – may or may not have been warranted. But the city's response was certainly calculated to have that effect.

It is not difficult to imagine the council discovering the overdue rent and chuckling over the advantage repossession would give them in negotiating with Irving over the pulp mill's rates.

Accordingly, Commissioner A.E. Hanson, city Controller Ronald Park, and Assessment Director L.A. Cooper drove out to the site, officially entered upon the watershed, and repossessed it in the name of the city. Then, on August 18, the city announced that Irving's lease had been cancelled for nonpayment of rent. It also announced that the door was open for negotiations.

The city then sat back to await the onset of negotiations with a company that would, it seemed reasonable to expect, be willing to give up a few of the advantages of the pulp mill water rates in order to regain the Little River watershed. But – perhaps because city governments change, and each new one has to relearn the lesson of how to get along with the Irving dinosaur – the city had badly misjudged its adversary. Clearly the city thought of itself as dealing with a normal corporation, one that decided its tactics by the balance book. But Irving's dinosaur was not so easily manipulated.

What Irving did was to ignore the proffered negotiations, to treat both deals as betrayals, and to issue a monumentally enraged public statement in which he withdrew his one hundred million dollar Chignecto Canal "commitment" on the grounds that these two actions by the city proved it was impossible to deal with the city fathers of Saint John.

"You can't do business with people who want only to oppose and attack you," he said, ignoring the fact that his own secretiveness suggested that these were the only kind of people around. It was, he said, "impossible to obtain co-operation and fair business dealings in respect to agreements with the city of Saint John. . . . Under the existing conditions, it would be ridiculous to consider new agreements with a city which, apparently, is more anxious to break contracts than to see progress."

Characteristically, Irving's statement dripped with outrage and pique. "We received the watershed rights," he complained, "before we started construction of the refinery. Now the refinery has been built, the money has been spent, and the city wants to break the agreement. How can you conduct business dealings in such an atmosphere?" Generalizing a bit, Irving unlimbered what has always been his biggest gun in disputes with governments – the veiled threat to pull his investment out of the area altogether. He had invested $80,000,000 in the area over the past three years, he said. "Now that the investments have been made and the industries are an accomplished fact, the city is attempting to repudiate the water agreement with Irving Pulp and Paper Limited and terminate the Little River watershed lease by Irving Refining Limited." What was an honest man to do under such circumstances?

As Irving had no doubt calculated, the ensuing publicity was mammoth, spectacular and nation-wide. Mayor Eric L. Teed tried to put a brave face on things, suggesting that the whole business was just a misunderstanding, but the city's position had been wrecked. The Little River lease was no longer useful as a lever in the water rates fight, and though that fight went all the way to the Supreme Court eventually, the city was beaten and knew it. Mayor Teed, for instance, publicly said he didn't think the city had a case. The Supreme Court agreed.

This incident gives rise to a number of reflections about the Irving empire and its power, but what is most immediately clear is the extent to which Irving can control the affairs of the government of Saint John, even though he is not directly involved in politics at all. Through three city administrations, every action the city council took with respect to Saint John's water supply problems was subject to an Irving veto. Partly because of his astute handling of publicity, partly because of his brillant legal and financial manoeuvering, and primarily because of the sheer weight of his presence in the city, Irving was able to force through and to retain concessions that were all but ruinous to the city. Was there ever any real possibility that Irving would pull his investments out of Saint John? It is impossible to be certain; at any rate, no one has ever tried to call his bluff.

Perhaps the single most important factor in Irving's ability to exercise his power so fluidly and expertly, however, is the nature of his control of the empire he created. One of the most consistent principles of action underlying Irving's policies has been the drive to own one hundred per cent, to have to consider no outside pressures when making decisions. Corporate control, of course, can be achieved with a good deal less than fifty-one per cent of a company; often a plurality is all that is necessary. Sometimes a consortium of owners can control a corporation by agreeing on basic policies. And sometimes a company or an individual can get a contract to manage the affairs of a corporation without actually owning any of its stock. But Irving is never happy with such an arrangement. It is clear that, to him, "control" means complete ownership and total control. His company, Engineering Consultants Limited, had the management contract for the giant smelter at Brunswick Mining and Smelting in the mid-sixties, for instance, and yet Irving said later that he had never had control. It is clear that he meant that there were other stockholders to answer to, as well as government representatives on the company's board of directors. The typical Irving company has a board of directors composed primarily of Irving, members of his family, and close associates; it issues no stock publicly and so has to make no annual reports public. Irving sees two advantages to this way of doing business. One is that corporate secrecy is much more easily maintained; there is no difficulty in discovering quite a lot about the affairs of a company which is listed on a stock exchange, but Irving's companies are required to list no information publicly beyond their officers. Thus it is well-nigh impossible to be certain which companies have been taken over by Irving or his subsidiaries; often the only concrete evidence is the presence of Irving lieutenants in the list of company officers.

A consideration that is often overlooked about this is that the combination of secrecy and staggering complexity which the Irving corporate structure exhibits can be a vitally important weapon. The near-impossibility of tracing lines of authority and responsibility within the structure makes it very difficult for adversaries to get a hook into an Irving company. Consider, for instance, the Kafkaesque frustration experienced by the Seafarers' International Union as it tried, in the summer of 1971, to get itself certified as bargaining agent for the crews of six Irving-operated ships.

The six ships were the *Irvingstream*, the *Irving Ours Polaire*, the *Irvingwood*, the *Aimé Gaudreau*, and two identified only by serial numbers, the *H-1060* and the *H-1070*. The workers on the ships believed – and the union said so in its application to the Canada Labour Relations Board – that they were employed by Kent Lines Limited. The Board's hearings were held in October and November of that year.

It turned out that the corporate structure was so complicated that not only did the workers and the union not know who employed the seamen on the six ships, but many of the management employees of the companies didn't know either. The ships were all owned and managed in such diverse and confusing ways that responsibility was impossible to pin down.

The *Irvingstream*, for instance, was wholly owned by Irving Oil Limited, but its ship's agent was Kent Lines. The *Irving Ours Polaire* was owned jointly by three companies – Kent Lines (sixteen shares), Universal Sales Limited (twelve shares) and J.D. Irving Limited (thirty-six shares). The J.D. Irving interest had been acquired only ten months before – and thus during the period relevant to the application – from Engineering Consultants Limited. The ship had been, in any case, on a twenty-year "bareboat charter" to Irving Oil since 1962 – and Kent Lines was its ship's agent.

The *Aimé Gaudreau*, similarly on charter to Irving Oil and managed by Kent Lines, was owned by four companies – Kent Lines (sixteen shares), Engineering Consultants (thirty-two shares), Universal Sales (four shares) and J.D. Irving (twelve shares). The two other boats, the *H-1060* and the *H-1070*, were wholly owned by Engineering Consultants and were normally on trip charters for Irving Oil. The only boat actually owned outright by Kent Lines, the *Irvingwood*, was also normally on charter to Irving Oil.

If that doesn't sound complicated enough, consider some of the other evidence offered at the hearings. Kent Lines acts as ship's agent for all six ships, but does so on a different basis for the ones owned by Engineering Consultants. On the vessels owned by, or on bareboat charter to, Irving Oil, it is the oil company rather than Kent Lines which handles personnel matters, with the payroll merely passing through the latter company; on the other hand, with respect to the two E.C.L.-owned boats, Kent Lines handles all the details of payroll, repair, supplies and personnel matters. But on those two boats, since it owns no part of them, it does not receive a share of profits, whereas it does in the case of the *Irving Ours Polaire* and the *Aimé Gaudreau*, in each of which it owns a one-fourth interest. Astonishingly, the masters of the two E.C.L.-owned ships are paid directly by Irving Oil, which apparently owns no part of them.

The impression of the seamen on all six vessels, in spite of all this, was that they were working for Kent Lines. Their notice of appointment had come on Kent Lines stationery, as did overtime statements. Payroll stubs were stamped "Kent Lines Limited." On documents filled out by the ships' masters and supplied to the Federal Department of Transport, Kent Lines was listed as the "Managing Owner" of all six vessels; the obvious conclusion is that even the Masters of the ships didn't know who owned them.

To further deepen the fog, many of the functions purportedly performed by Kent Lines are in fact performed by employees of Irving Oil. The personnel superintendent of Irving

Oil, for instance, apparently serves, *de facto*, the same function for Kent Lines. And the Supply and Transportation Manager of Irving Oil seems to be the man who actually runs all six vessels. He testified to the Board that he had authority to hire and fire – had, in fact, once fired the master of the *Irvingwood* – and that the authority came from Arthur Irving, Vice-President of Irving Oil.

Of all the companies involved, the only one that publicly claims to be engaged in the business of operating vessels is Kent Lines. In their annual returns, Irving Oil says its business is petroleum products, E.C.L. says it is an engineering consulting firm, Universal Sales is listed as an automobile dealership, and so forth. So who's minding the store? The Chairman of the Labour Relations Board, J.J. Quinlan, blew the foghorn in the Board's report: "On the facts which have been adduced, there is no argument that the persons concerned in the application are employees," – a conclusion which must have relieved them – "The question is whether or not the Respondent is the employer on the six vessels concerned."

Of course, if you follow the ownership chain up through the corporate maze, it's clear that all the companies are fundamentally the same company, that in the long run all the seamen involved work for K.C. Irving Limited. Every one of the companies involved is owned outright or controlled by that corporation. But the complexity of the corporate structure made it impossible for the union to decide whom to deal with. As Quinlan pointed out, the union found itself in a pretty "disadvantageous" position, "due to lack of information which it was only able to obtain at considerable expense by full hearings and examination under oath of officials and employees of the various companies." In other words, the only way they could find out who they were working for was by going to court. The Board report observed, in a model of understatement, "this does not appear to be equitable." It went on to suggest some reforms: "In the view of the Board this case is a classic example of a situation which could best be taken care of by specific legislation whereby one of the corporate entities, depending on the evidence adduced, may be declared to be the employer for collective bargaining purposes."

Without such a law, however, the Board found itself unable to do much. It decided that only the employees aboard the *Irvingwood* – the boat actually owned by Kent Lines – could be certified as members of the Seafarers' Union to bargain collectively with Kent Lines. The employees aboard the other five boats were left to cope with the situation as best they might: if you don't know who you're working for, you can't organize or bargain collectively. It's a situation that Franz Kafka would have admired.

There is another advantage to private, secret ownership of a complex structure; it has to do with freedom of action. "When you go public," Irving has said, "you have certain rules you have to go by. Those may not make it the most convenient way of accomplishing what you set out to do. You can take a calculated risk if you only have to account to yourself." It is this principle of complete ownership, in other words, which is largely responsible for the extent to which Irving's personality has been imprinted on his corporations. There are no stockholders to restrain management from taking chances, no middle-management to make decisions on the basis of maintaining the lowest possible profile. It is traditional in an Irving company that every employee, from the vice-president to the pulp-cutter or gas station attendant, is directly responsible to K.C. Irving himself, and the stories of Irving suddenly appearing at a gas station or a remote lumber camp are so common that there is clearly a basis in truth for them.

This principle of complete ownership and domination is visible in the very earliest dealings of the Irving corporations. During the depression, for instance, Irving's father died and left J.D. Irving Limited to his family – to his wife, his daughters Lou Dorothy and Marion Robertson, and to his sons, John Herbert and Kenneth Colin. Within a few years K.C., whose aggressive tactics, at a time when lumber companies were dropping like flies, scared the rest of the family, had bought them out and acquired effective control of J.D. Irving Limited.

But Irving did not consolidate his own personal land holdings in J.D. Irving Limited – nor did he use it as the vehicle to buy the New Brunswick Railway's million acres of New Brunswick timberland – because the estate was not yet entirely cleared up, and control might conceivably not yet be complete. He did not turn over his own land to the company until 1962, when the last claimant to the estate of his father finally died, leaving him the sole remaining executor, and the estate was finally wound up. Only then, it seems, was Irving satisfied that he had what he could call control.

That urge toward total control is probably closely related to another, equally fundamental, pattern in the Irving business method. Called by economists "vertical integration", it is the practice of acquiring companies or industries which are either your suppliers or whom you supply, working toward a complete chain from raw material to consumer. Almost all really cohesive business empires are built on this principle, and Irving's is no exception. The logic of it is easy to see, though the details are often complex and sometimes the connections are not immediately apparent. Beginning with automobiles, for instance, the entrepreneur goes into gas and oil retailing because the gas and oil are consumed by the cars. He goes into real estate and the construction business – as Irving did immediately after his move to Saint John in the late twenties and early thirties – because you need land to build gas stations on, and companies to build them. He goes into hardware because the building company needs supplies, as do the automobiles. He goes into trucking to transport his oil, and into the shipping business, and into the shipbuilding and drydock business to maintain a fleet of oil tankers. He opens a refinery to supply the service stations, and a superport to supply the refinery and the tankers. He buys bus companies because they use gas, and begins building bus bodies to supply the bus companies. He buys a veneer plant to supply veneer for the bus bodies.

The same logic applies to the building up of the lumbering and pulp and paper empire. Each step in the integration not only eliminates a possible source of opposition or friction, but provides opportunities for the sort of corporate complication that is represented by the Bahamian oil company's role in the refinery's account book. After a while the profits are lost in the maze, and the whole becomes an exercise in keeping funds and materials in constant motion, never allowing profit to accumulate, but reinvesting it before its growth slows.

The process is one from which, as it accelerates, it becomes increasingly difficult to escape, and one wonders about the feelings of an Irving, whose opportunities (and desire) for relaxation became, as the empire grew, fewer and fewer. The commitment to investing money effectively is a never-ending one: if one dollar is invested well, it returns two, which have to be invested better. And any attempt to stop, to put the money someplace safe and stable and undemanding, impugns the validity of the whole process. The average man's notion of what is entailed in "making it" financially stretches no further than an unlimited income and no obligations. But for an Irving, for any man who dedicates his life to the efficient investment of capital, that "income" is raw material. Beyond a certain point it stops being privilege and becomes obligation – and though it carries power and privilege and pleasure with it, it clearly is primarily obligation.

Such reflections lead directly to the central consideration in any study of a phenomenon like Irving, which is: why? The question sounds facetious, but it is in fact deadly serious. To understand why men like Irving – and there are many of them – do what they do would be to understand the most fundamental and important aspects of the economic system we live in. And that the answer is far from easy, the question far from superficial, is made clear by Irving's own attempts to deal with it. What is surely some of the most fascinating dialogue in the history of business in Canada occurred during the Senate Mass Media Committee's interrogation of Irving as to why he had bought all those newspapers in the first place.

At the outset, it was stated clearly that none of the newspapers were very efficient as money-making concerns, either when Irving acquired them or thereafter, and, accordingly, one of the main lines of questioning by various interrogators centred around the question Senator Prowse voiced at the outset: "Would you mind telling me why you would bother to own newspapers, radio and television stations, when you don't participate in the operation of them and you take no money out of them?" In the early stages, Irving's answers were facile and untroubled; it was clear that the question did not bother him. "Well," he said, clarifying an earlier, almost incomprehensible answer, "I can understand that it would look a little peculiar to people living in some other parts of Canada, but it is the only way I know to get along in New Brunswick and in the Maritimes, and to retain control of some part of the activity." He went on to explain that at least one motive involved the fact that any money generated by the newspapers would be – had, he said, been – reinvested in New Brunswick and not outside.

A few moments later, Irving responded to a question from Yves Fortier, the committee's counsel, by raising the issue himself, as though it were bothering him. "Well, now," he said, "I will have to go back to the early part of your question. You said when I purchase companies or start companies, it is for the purpose of making money."

"Yes."

"I think," Irving said, being sure, "that is what you said."

"That is what I said. Yes."

"Yes; well, I have purchased companies and started companies to create activity, not necessarily to make money. They might never make money but they would create a certain amount of activity. I would have invested the money far better if I had invested it just straight to make money directly in the stock market, perhaps, or something else." It is apparent that Irving sees investing money merely to make more money as vaguely silly, that he thinks stock market speculation is a bit beneath him. His goals are more complex. But it is also apparent that he himself doesn't see clearly what they are; "to create activity" is a singularly unenlightening phrase.

Fortier was soon back at it again. "I am genuinely curious," he said, "about your reasons for acquiring newspapers in New Brunswick. I do not think you answered Senator Prowse earlier and he kept his question in abeyance and I would like to return. Why do you acquire newspapers?"

Prepared as he was, Irving was clearly stumped. "Well, I think that – why do I, I would have to ask myself the same question."

Fortier tried again: "Someone once said about mountain climbing – because they are there."

Irving was unconvinced. "Perhaps."

At this point Senator Davey, in the chair, intervened. "Would you like to answer that question?"

It was obvious that Irving would have liked to be able to answer it. "You know, that is pretty hard to answer."

"I think," Davey suggested, "it is a fair question."

Irving apparently thought so too. But self-examination has never been his forte. "All right. Could you say, 'why do you buy something else? Why do you buy a ship or something else?' I suppose there is a very good reason; there is the opportunity of creating earnings and that sort of thing, rounding out your . . . increasing your activity . . . in the province and your interest, I would say." The answer seemed to strike him as unsatisfying. "But it is not the answer you are looking for, I do not think."

"I am not looking for any answer, Mr. Irving, any specific answer," Fortier said, staying with it. "I am looking for your answer."

"Well, you know, it is kind of hard to tell you that."

And it was clearly hard for Irving to tell himself. The phrases that come closest, it seems, aren't finally economic at all, but rest on some other basis. "Rounding out your . . . increasing your activity."

Later that afternoon, as though everyone recognized that some significant light was being generated – though nobody knew quite what it illuminated – the subject came around again. At the very end of the session, Senator Douglas D. Everett asked for yet another consideration of the question of financial return. He said that it was his understanding that Irving did not buy the papers "for financial return."

Irving hastened to set the record straight, as though he had been accused of some species of folly. "Oh, I did not say that. I did not so far up to now. I did not buy them for the purpose of acquiring dividends. I will say that immediately. Dividends are dividends. But I did not say I did not buy them for the purpose of them being profitable."

Everett pursued the matter, clearly sensing some discomfort around the question. He agreed that he could imagine someone prepared to wait a long time for profits – but profit would still be the main point. "There is nothing loaded," he said, "in somebody saying to you, 'Mr. Irving, are you interested in financial return on these newspapers that you buy?' "

It is clear – it was clear throughout the afternoon – that the simplest course for Irving would have been to say that he bought the papers for long-term financial return. It would have closed the subject. But, interestingly, Irving chose not to take that avenue. K.C. Irving Limited, he repeated, had received no financial return from the newspapers. Everett stick-handled. "I am asking whether you are interested in that or whether you, in fact, buy these papers for social reasons."

"Most everything you do," Irving replied, "has a certain amount of social reason in it, but I bought those papers, very well, to make businesses out of them. And what is a business?"

Everett was not about to give up. "The question is simple. I just say, 'Do you buy for financial return?'"

"Nobody," Irving answered, clearly nettled, "has got any financial return yet out of those papers. Is that clear?"

"That is right."

"So K.C. Irving did not buy them for immediate financial return."

Everett, aware that Irving was not going to take the easy way out, then referred to "another reason that we have not been able to probe, that has to do with your big, vast holdings in New Brunswick, or your feelings as to how New Brunswick should run. That is what is important to us in committee."

49

Everett tried once more. "If you say that it is financial return. . . . "

Irving made one last attempt to explain that "financial return" was not a phrase that matched his sense of his own motives. "I believe that the newspaper business and newspapers, if well run, are good business. So I am interested in them from that standpoint, and, too, seeing that good people are in charge."

Everett was not ready to interpret that. "Good business" clearly meant only one thing to him. "So then, we can say that you are interested, albeit in the long range, in the long range financial return?"

Irving gave up. "Yes. I am." To pursue the distinction between what he apparently saw as his own long-range goals and Everett's unwillingness to look beyond finances would clearly reintroduce the possibility that he had acquired the newspapers in order to manipulate the media in the province to his own advantage, a possibility it would be better to avoid. So he let the unsatisfying answer stand. The afternoon session was adjourned.

The implications of this long cross-examination are fascinating. Surely the sensible course for a man in Irving's position would have been to allow the Senate to continue to believe that his motives were purely the making of money: yet he refused, through the whole long session, to do so. It seems clear that Fortier's "genuine curiosity" stirred his own, that the question is one which does in fact fascinate him, and that he is not used to talking about such matters.

In fact, Irving sounds – it may be a farfetched analogy, but it is an astonishingly rewarding one – more like an artist, a novelist or poet or painter, than he does like a businessman. One does not expect an artist to be able to explain, for instance, why he puts a blob of blue in the lower right-hand corner of his canvas; it is his job to know that it should be there, not to be able to explain why. It may well be, on the other hand, that an aesthetician or critic can explain – once the blue blob is in place – why it is necessary, in order to make the painting complete and satisfying; but the ability to explain the principles doesn't imply any ability to produce the painting in the first place. Just so, Irving cannot explain – and ought not to be expected to explain – exactly why he buys one company and not another; why he expands the pulp mill and not the bus line. He may not even be able to explain the theory of vertical integration – but the theory is itself an explanation of what he and people like him actually do. The explainer, the economist, probably can't do what Irving does; understanding the physics of vibrating strings and playing the violin are two very different things.

The analogy with an artist goes even further. Just as the artist often refuses to discuss or think about really ultimate aims (What is art for? What purpose does it serve in the ultimate human scheme of things?), so Irving is the furthest thing from a economic theorizer. To "create activity", to make "good business", is as close as he can come to the elaborate abstractions of economic theory – and as close as he has to come.

Moreover – and perhaps most important – what he's doing satisfies Irving in exactly the same way that the artist's product satisfies him. Some hint of this can be seen in the words he chooses to explain why he buys things. "The opportunity of creating earnings and that sort of thing, rounding out your . . . increasing your activity . . . ". Exactly the kind of explanation you might expect from that artist. The blue blob "rounds out" the painting. In fact, Irving's life work boils down to the construction of a corporate structure that will be as elegant, symmetrical, efficient – as satisfying – as possible. And the criteria for deciding whether a company fits into that orderly structure are very similar to the criteria employed by a poet choosing a word or a painter choosing a shape and a colour. Yes, the poet's sentence must make sense, the painter's picture may have to create an image – but in each case the choice must also contribute to the creation of the whole. Just so, Irving's company may have to make money, turn a dividend, or increase his activity: but at the level he is working at the relations between the new element and the old structure are so complex that it becomes, as surely as the poet's or the painter's choice, a matter of feeling and genius.

There is, however, a difference that is as important as all the similarities. Irving's materials, unlike the painter's pigments or the poet's words, are the lives of human beings. It is this that makes the game so dangerous, the stakes so high, the issues finally moral rather than aesthetic. No one thinks of the study of aesthetic criteria in art as a matter of life and death. But for the poor and dispossessed of eastern Canada as well as for the small businessman, the woodlot owner, the dockworker, the study of Irving's style is the study of their own destiny. We are the chickens in the old saw about the elephant dancing among the chickens and shouting, "it's every man for himself." Only in our case it's a dinosaur. And, in any case, choreography can be a pretty important study among us chickens.

Another, equally important, distinction between Irving's creature and the creation of an artist is that the dinosaur goes on growing and changing and acting and finally acquires a will of its own, a direction, a sense of purpose. Shambling out of the reach of its creator, the gigantic monstrosity does represent a dinosaur much more than a painting: huge, at the end of a long evolutionary process, concerned almost entirely with self-preservation, invulnerable and dense, its bloated and ungainly shape makes it incapable of much more than ravaging the immediate area to support its existence.

And as with the dinosaur, history is clearly against the Irving monster. There are not many places left in the world where such a gigantic thing could be put together, not many places where it could survive. Like the dinosaur, it cannot adapt to change, and as the planet wobbles on its axis and the climate cools, as the little warm-blooded animals appear and start eating its eggs, it will die, lapsing back into a mere corporation like others – quasi-governmental, run by cautious, sensible middle managers driven only by their own instincts toward self-preservation. And the world will be a safer, if a bit duller, place.

CHAPTER TWO

The Buses of Saint John

The manner in which the Common Council has dealt with the bus franchise," declared an obviously indignant K.C. Irving, "certainly discourages anyone from increasing investments or establishing new industries in Saint John." It was a rebuke that was to become characteristic of Irving, but the first time the citizens of Saint John heard it was in the summer of 1936, in one of the early rounds of a fight over Saint John's public transportation system that was to last twelve years, involve every weapon in the formidable Irving arsenal, and end – typically – in a victory for Irving that was, by the time the final verdict was in, an almost empty one.

What bothered Irving in 1936 was that not only had the common council failed even to consider his application for a bus franchise, but, in a resolution the mayor said was "railroaded through", it had awarded the franchise to the Saint John industrialist's chief competitor, Halifax entrepreneur Fred C. Manning. It was Irving's first major encounter with the city fathers and he had been outmanoeuvred. Even more galling, he had been outmanoeuvred in his own home town by an outsider. Nor was it the last time Irving was to lose a round to the flamboyant Mr. Manning, who was to be his opposition in the twelve-year fight over the civic transit franchise, a fight that would occur in law courts, the common council, the legislature, back rooms throughout the province, and board rooms as far away as New York City.

Though the value of the prize had diminished considerably by the time Irving finally walked off with it in 1948, the education that he had received over the dozen years was worth almost any expense. The roots of Irving's later attitudes toward foreign investment, politicians, governments, competition, verbal contracts and business secrecy can all be found in the transit franchise fight. And all the characteristic weapons of Irving's financial and legal warfare were forged and their use refined in this arena, beginning with the thinly-veiled threat to pull his economic activity out of Saint John and continuing through the use of harassing injunctions and finally the exercise of political influence. Almost equally important, a good part of Irving's reputation for tenacity, doggedness, and long memory – a reputation which was to make many later fights unnecessary – derives from the way, time and again during the thirties and forties, Irving bounced off the ropes and came back stronger than ever.

In 1936 Irving had been in Saint John for ten years. During that time he had built one of the largest Ford dealerships in the Maritimes, the nine-year-old Irving Oil company was selling gasoline at about one hundred garages throughout the Maritimes, and that same year he had consolidated six bus companies into the S.M.T. System, the largest bus line in the Maritimes. The bus franchise for Saint John would round out the public transportation system he had so painstakingly put together over the past two years. Moreover, it was a matter of pride: Saint John was Irving's own turf. As he portentously pointed out to the councillors, "we have chosen to establish the head offices of our various companies in Saint John." It would scarcely do to have your chief competitor – an outsider from Halifax, at that – set up shop in your own back yard.

But the most characteristic thing about Irving's response was that it was a response conceived and delivered in anger and pique; unlike the practice of most corporations, which do not allow pride and a sense of justice to interfere with the balance book, Irving has always given free rein to his highly-honed sense of justice. The common council – in collaboration with Manning – had been unjust to the Irving interests. Such an act could not be allowed to go unchallenged. Nor was it; in fact, Irving's reactions to such skullduggery formed, it seems clear, the continuing motif of the fight, and served to keep the Irving interests engaged long after other companies might have either given up or seen that the game was no longer worth the candle, that the bus franchise was not nearly the prize in 1948 that it had seemed in the mid-thirties.

At the beginning, the franchise was the property of the New Brunswick Power Company, owned by Federal Light and Traction Company of New York. The franchise had been exclusive until January 1934; the Power Company ran twenty-three miles of streetcar tracks, thirty-four cars – almost all of which, in 1936, were in severe states of disrepair – and two buses, which it had bought in 1934. But, in the spring of 1935, the Power Company announced that it was for sale and offered the first option to the City of Saint John. John M. Robinson, a prestigious Saint John bond broker who was negotiating for the Power Company, told the city councillors that the company was faced with the alternative of selling or making large expenditures on its generating plant. While the worst of the depression was over, Federal Light and Traction nevertheless were reluctant to commit the capital necessary to modernize the obsolescent equipment operated by their marginally profitable New Brunswick subsidiary. "It is felt by the company," said Robinson, "that rather than make an additional investment in the generating plant it would prefer to offer the business to the city, so that all the services could be operated and controlled under one management to the greater benefit of all concerned, cutting out the duplication of service poles, wires and equipment of various kinds."

It seemed a reasonable suggestion. For more than a decade the city had been operating its own publicly owned Civic Hydro Company in competition with New Brunswick Power.

Each company had its own generating facilities and distribution network, and both systems were making a modest profit. But the New Brunswick Power Company also operated a gas manufacturing and distribution network and an obsolete street railway system, both of which were losing money – and insisted on selling all three systems as a package.

After a brief debate on the proposal, the councillors decided that they needed more information to reach a decision and so in June they resolved to have the company's assets appraised by the Toronto consulting firm of Clarkson, Gordon, Dillworth, Guilfoyle, and Nash. When the city receives the consultant's report, said Mayor James W. Brittain, we will evaluate it and hold a plebiscite.

By January 1936 it seemed probable that the consultants would recommend that the city purchase the New Brunswick Power Company, integrate the electric generating and distribution system into its own Civic Hydro and dispose of the gas generating and distribution system and the street railway to private companies. Irving, having just assembled the profitable S.M.T. System, was in a good position to see that with modern buses and good management, civic transit in Saint John could be a very profitable business. Consequently, in early January 1936, Louis McC. Ritchie, Irving's long-time friend and counsel, wrote to common council on behalf of the S.M.T. System requesting a conference with Mayor Brittain and the council about the possibility of awarding a franchise to the Irving company. Council Clerk Henry D. Hopkins then telephoned Ritchie to say that the council would be pleased to discuss the application, but suggested that they wait for the consultant's report; and Mayor Brittain suggested in a subsequent conversation with Ritchie that since he was planning to retire and since the civic elections would be coming up in a couple of months, it might be better to postpone discussions on a matter of such importance until the new mayor and council were in office. Certainly, agreed Ritchie, and he sat back to await the report and the April elections, no doubt confident of the outcome of the discussions. Meanwhile, the Clarkson, Gordon Report was presented to council at the beginning of March and recommended, as expected, that the city purchase the New Brunswick Power Company for $3,250,000, integrate the electric distribution system with that of Civic Hydro, improve the gas manufacturing plant and phase out the street railway system over the next five years in favour of a private company. It was a good deal. The Power Company valued its assets at $5,000,000 but was willing to sell to the city for the recommended price. But the city was not in a position to jump at it. "This is a question that should not be decided by snap judgment," said the *Evening Times-Globe* in a front page editorial accompanying the report. "Three of the five members of the Council, which ordered the survey, and which engaged in the preliminary discussion with the Power Company, may not be in Council after the civic election on April 13. The Mayor definitely has decided to retire, and two of the commissioners are standing for re-election. Hence it would be only good business for the matter to be deferred until the new mayor and council are in power." So the decision to purchase the Power Company was put off until after the election.

For a number of reasons, the election turned out to be a lacklustre campaign: no clear issues emerged and one council hopeful's attempt to make an issue of the Power Company purchase proposal failed. The two commissioners up for re-election were re-elected and D.L. MacLaren was chosen mayor by acclamation. But perhaps one reason nobody much cared was that under a civic government reorganization scheme eight "councillors" would be elected to replace the present four "commissioners" in November. It was a caretaker council with a six month mandate. It did not act on the Power Company's offer; the summer wore on and the complaints of riders on the city's lumbering and uncomfortable street cars continued. The Power Company once again announced plans to gradually replace some of their thirty-year-old trams with buses, but that was nothing new. As any serious thought of the city purchasing the Power Company faded further into the past, it began to look very much like the city would have to live with its old trams, broken roads and traffic congestion for some years to come.

Meanwhile Irving was patiently awaiting the outcome of the November elections, confident that since he had already signified his interest to the council he would be included in any discussions of the transportation franchise question. But Fred Manning was also aware of the situation in Saint John and Fred Manning was not a patient man. Nor, unlike Irving, was he politically inexperienced. Following a rumoured secret visit to the city in mid-July, Manning hired lawyer W.A. Ross to represent his interests in dealings with the council. Ross may not have been the best lawyer in Saint John, but as county secretary he certainly knew the mood of the council and had ready access to the councillors. At once bold and experienced in the ways of civic government, Manning laid his plans carefully. Just prior to a routine council meeting planned for July 27 Ross took Commissioner George Ellis into his confidence. Ellis agreed to introduce the resolution Ross suggested to him at the council meeting that afternoon. Ross then privately explained his plan to the other two councillors about to attend the meeting. Only Mayor MacLaren was surprised when Commissioner Ellis began the meeting by proposing that the city award Maritime Transit (Manning's firm) a franchise to run buses in the city for the next forty years.

As soon as the resolution was read Ross announced that he would like to appear before council not as the county secretary but as the solicitor for Maritime Transit Limited. Clearly astonished, the mayor listened in silence as Ross described the company's plans for a modern transportation system for the city and the three commissioners nodded in agreement.

Maritime Transit, said Ross, would make an immediate expenditure of more than $100,000 in "new buses of the latest and most modern type." The company already had four modern buses in the city ready to start operating as soon as permission was obtained from council. Another fifteen were waiting to be brought in and within a few weeks the company would have twenty-five to thirty new buses in operation in the city.

"I still think we should go into this more fully instead of putting it through today," offered the mayor to the three enthusiastic commissioners. "I hold no brief for the New Brunswick Power Company," he continued, "but it is a large taxpayer and employs many citizens." Ross retorted that it was evident that the Power Company had no intention of making any large expenditures to institute a bus service. "Many parts of the city are not now served by the street railway and the public in general wishes a bus service." Moreover, he argued, "tourists laugh at our present street railway cars."

"The directors will be Saint John men and the employees will be 100 per cent local men," declared Ross, although he declined to say just who the directors were or for that matter reveal the name of the "large outside concern" that was financially backing the company. He added that although the company had not yet applied for incorporation it would do so at once. But the details could be worked out later, he assured the commissioners; and the resolution was passed, with the mayor casting the sole opposing vote. Manning's audacity had been rewarded, but the reaction was not long in coming. Later that day, the vice-president and general manager of the New Brunswick Power Company, W.P. Southard, reacted with surprise and declared that his company "had no intention of going out of the transportation business in Saint John. I think it strange," he added, "that action such as taken at City Hall today should have been taken without the courtesy of a hearing being given the New Brunswick Power Company." But that was only the beginning.

Having recovered his composure, the next day he announced that the Power Company would "fight to the finish" to protect its investment. "This franchise is not a franchise at all," he continued, "but a blanket order to Maritime Transit to go ahead and ruin the other fellow's business. The worst feature of this fiasco is the manner in which it was put over by the council, with no advance notice and with nobody having an opportunity of a hearing. Furthermore, it doesn't seem reasonable for the council to give a blanket order to somebody it knows nothing about." Nevertheless, Ross adamantly refused to reveal the names of the principals of Maritime Transit. "I can't tell you anything at this time," he said. But the newspapers were already speculating that F.C. Manning was behind the company.

On Thursday, amid a flurry of front page editorials condemning the "enormity of the blunder", asking if there ever was "a more pitiful exhibition of unbusinesslike management and utter disregard for the public interest", the council met in an attempt to clarify the issue. Mayor MacLaren had decided, upon reflection, that the resolution had been "railroaded" through council by Commissioners Ellis, Walsh and Wigmore and he said so when the meeting opened. "It was a very high-handed piece of business," declared the mayor. Commissioner Massie, absent from the meeting on Monday, stated that he would never have voted for it and enquired if the motion could be rescinded. Meanwhile, Cyrus F. Inches, one of New Brunswick's foremost corporation lawyers, who was acting for the Power Company, was applying that afternoon to New Brunswick Chief Justice J.B.M. Baxter for an injunction to restrain the city and Commissioners Ellis, Walsh and Wigmore from acting under the franchise resolution.

And an indignant K.C. Irving and his solicitor, Louis Ritchie, addressed the council meeting. Irving pointed out to the council that he had applied for a franchise last January "when it was known proposed plans included the abandonment of the street car service and substitution of buses. By agreement with Mayor Brittain and His Worship Mayor MacLaren our application was allowed to stand in abeyance and we felt that as we were complying with the wishes of the mayor of the city our position was secure and we would have an opportunity of being heard before any action was taken with regard to the franchise." Clearly – and characteristically – Irving was not only indignant, but hurt. By playing according to the rules, he had set himself up as an all too easy target for the wily and more experienced Manning. "We believe the way in which this whole matter has been handled has been most unfair to ourselves," said Irving. "As citizens we should be entitled to at least an opportunity of presenting our proposal. We do not believe that any one taxpayer should receive more consideration than another but for your information we would like to state the following figures relating to the operations of our companies in Saint John." All citizens are equal, but some, of course, are more equal than others. And Irving, using for the first time a tactic that was to become a regular part of his repertoire, stated the figures: "Our yearly taxes exceed $20,-000. We employ 212 persons . . . and our yearly payroll is in excess of $247,000. . . . I might add that we have chosen to establish the head offices of our various companies in Saint John. These companies operate throughout the Maritime Provinces and employ 482 additional persons, making a total of 694 on our payrolls. I might also add that actions such as the manner in which the Common Council has dealt with the bus franchise," continued Irving, turning the screw a little more, "certainly would discourage anyone from increasing investments or establishing new industries in Saint John. It is our opinion that in fairness to all concerned, the resolution granting the franchise should be rescinded," concluded Irving, "and that all should be given a fair opportunity of discussing the matter." Whereupon the mayor sprang to his feet and said, "We had the city solicitor in here, Mr. Irving, and we are awaiting his opinion as to whether we can rescind that resolution."

The next day, the city solicitor said that he thought the resolution could be rescinded and Commissioner Ellis, who had moved the original motion, said that he was now ready to move a rescinding motion. "I realize," said the commissioner, "that I acted hastily in moving the resolution without first advising the mayor of my intentions. I want it to be understood that I have nothing against the New Brunswick Power Company or any other organization doing business in Saint John."

But Ross wasn't about to let the commissioners off that easily. If the common council rescinded the resolution that it passed Monday, giving Maritime Transit a forty-year franchise he said his company would institute a damage action against the city and "fight it through the courts, even to the Privy Council if necessary." He added that there was "big money" behind Maritime Transit and that the men for whom he was acting – he still refused to reveal their names – were ready to fight the rescinding of the motion with the best legal talent available.

Nevertheless, on August 10, council rescinded the motion it had passed two weeks before, with Mayor MacLaren and Commissioners Ellis and Massie supporting the motion and Commissioners Walsh and Wigmore opposing. And with that the controversy died down, as all parties consulted their lawyers. Common council returned to routine business, while Mayor MacLaren denied that he had been in conference with the Power Company and the Irving Oil Company. "I have not been in conference with two other companies," he told Commissioner Walsh. W.P. Southard, general manager of the Power Company, announced that his company would be replacing its trams with buses and denied that he had disposed of the street railway rights to K.C. Irving. Meanwhile, Ross announced that Maritime Transit planned to go ahead with a bus service, and that it had financial backing from United Service Corporation (F.C. Manning's company). But then everyone knew that anyway.

Then on Saturday afternoon, October 3, with the issue all but forgotten, Commissioner Walsh sold the Maritime Transit Company, for one hundred dollars, an easement for a bus stop on North Market Street in the heart of the city. At the commissioner's direction a works crew painted lines on the street and put up signs just after midnight. By Sunday morning the company had two buses carrying passengers throughout the city and it was rumoured that more were on the way from Halifax. Company solicitor Ross explained, "the buses are here for inspection purposes – so far – so the people can see what we have to offer." The mayor consulted with the city solicitor. Meanwhile Ross, wearing his other hat as county secretary, read the commissioners a letter from Louis Ritchie saying that he was interested in applying for a franchise when the question came up again. Attached to Ritchie's letter were copies of the letters he had sent to council in January and July saying the same thing. Ross explained to council that he had never received the letter mailed in January – despite the fact that it had been published in the evening newspaper – and that he had replied to the July letter on his own authority, suggesting that Mr. Ritchie take the matter up with the provincial government. Ritchie's and Irving's education was proceeding apace: now they were relearning the old adage that it's difficult to fight City Hall.

All that month the Maritime Transit Company buses continued to operate throughout the city, still carrying signs reading "These buses are for inspection purposes only." But following the defeat of all of the former commissioners in the civic elections held on November 3, the company no doubt thought it was time to force the new council into a decision. Four days later, a little over a month after the buses had first appeared in the city, the company announced that it was beginning commercial operations and would begin charging fares. Mayor MacLaren said that the company was operating in "direct defiance" of common council and he was studying the possibility of court action. "I consider that the methods of the Maritime Transit Company from the very start have been high-handed," he declared. Meanwhile, the New Brunswick Power Company announced that it too would start a bus service, leasing two buses from Irving's S.M.T. System until it could purchase its own. Wendell W. Rogers, President of S.M.T., denied that his company would start its own bus service. With all the dignity of a virgin in a whore house, Rogers announced that his company "would respect the wishes of Common Council and the rights of the New Brunswick Power Company."

Sorting its way through the legal tangle, the Power Company finally applied for an injunction to prohibit Maritime Transit from operating buses in the city. On December 15, the injunction was granted and the next day the M.T.C. buses were taken off the streets. But the fight had just begun.

At this point the New Brunswick Power Company, the dog

in Saint John's manger, was losing money on its street railway system, but despite its announced plans to the contrary was reluctant to make more than a token gesture toward modernizing the system or replacing the trams with buses. On the other hand, it refused to sell its transportation system to a company that would modernize it. The Power Company was still eager to sell all of its assets, but not separately.

This posed a difficult problem for Irving, who now more than ever wanted to add the potentially profitable civic transportation franchise to the successful S.M.T. System. Moreover, the outcome of the legal battle which followed Manning's grab for the franchise remained in doubt. Maritime Transit was planning to appeal Chief Justice Baxter's decree restraining it from operating in competition with the Power Company. If the appeal was successful, Irving would lose the franchise before he had ever actually joined the fight for it.

Irving had learned one lesson well: doing it in private is better than doing it in public. So, while the city and the New Brunswick Power Company were publicly battling the Manning interests, Irving quietly journeyed to New York to confer with the president of Federal Light and Traction, owners of the Power Company. The negotiations were successful and by early February Irving had an option to purchase the New Brunswick Power Company. On February 11, 1937, the same day argument began in the Maritime Transit appeal in Fredericton, three Saint John bond houses, Eastern Securities Limited, T.M. Bell and Company and Irving, Brennan and Company, appeared before the annual meeting of the city-owned Civic Hydro Commission to propose the amalgamation of the two parallel systems. The consortium proposed that the city either buy the distribution network and generating plant of the Power Company and amalgamate them with its own Civic Hydro or, alternatively, sell Civic Hydro to a new third company which would amalgamate them. The consortium pointed out the numerous financial benefits that would accrue to the city from such an amalgamation. But it wasn't until close to the end of the proposal that the consortium noted that should it choose to exercise its option it "intended to organize a company to take over the street railway owned by the New Brunswick Power Company and maintain a modern and efficient transportation system in Saint John." Moreover, the consortium promised to spend $750,000 to do it. It was the long way around, but would meet the terms of the Power Company, and, most important, give Irving the transportation franchise.

The city greeted the proposal with considerable interest and decided to hire Gordon Kribs, a Toronto consulting engineer, to appraise it and advise the city. Two months later, after an apparently exhaustive examination, the Kribs Report – as it came to be known – recommended that the city proceed with the amalgamation of the distribution and generating systems and scrap the street car service, selling the transportation franchise "to a group willing to conduct an efficient bus service."

The Civic Hydro Commission advised the city to accept the Kribs Report recommendations and purchase the Power Company's assets. Faced with heavy expenditures to modernize its system, the Power Company affirmed its desire to sell to the city. And the bond dealers – led by Irving's close friend and financial colleague Frank Brennan – met behind closed doors to urge Bouctouche-born Premier Dysart and members of his Liberal cabinet to encourage the city to make the purchase. But the city demurred. The $3,250,000 price was too much for the depression-burdened shoulders of the Saint John taxpayer, reasoned the council. "It would not be in the best interests of the City of Saint John." In a front page editorial on September 2, the *Evening Times-Globe* commended the city's decision, noting, "there has been no public clamour or demand in this city for such a purchase and this has been true in the face of an intensive campaign of propaganda, carried on for some months, having such an outcome as its object." Irving was learning how to use propaganda, too. But the newspapers were still a bit too independent of his power or influence.

For the next two years the issue was dormant. Manning had lost his appeal that spring and it was clear that neither the city nor the courts would permit him to snatch the transportation franchise away from the Power Company. It was equally clear that the Power Company would not sell its transportation franchise separately to Irving, nor could Irving afford, or arrange, a deal to purchase all of the company's assets.

One year later, in September 1938, Irving again travelled to New York to initiate secret negotiations with the president of Federal Light and Traction, hoping to arrange the sale of the company's transportation franchise. The secret negotiations continued irregularly for eight months until May 1939, when they culminated in a tentative agreement that was reduced to writing but not signed. Federal Light and Traction agreed that if it sold its street railway system and franchise, it would sell them to Irving's S.M.T. (Eastern) Limited. But the company wasn't ready to sell yet. If everyone thought Saint John's transportation system could make money with new equipment and good management, no doubt the New Brunswick Power Company thought so too. And now that capital was more readily available, the company was in a position to modernize its own system. Accordingly, W.P. Southard, company vice-president and general manager, went to common council in mid-January 1940 with a proposal to replace the company's street cars with buses. But for all its eagerness to rid the city of street cars, the city, recalling the legal entanglements of three years ago, asked for a clarification of its authority to approve such a move. Moreover, as several councillors pointed out, if the city was talking about buses, it should give everyone interested in applying for the franchise an opportunity to be heard.

Again confronted by increasing complexities raised by the issue and preoccupied with war demands, common council didn't get around to calling for proposals from interested parties until the fall of 1941. On September 19, the common council clerk was directed to notify all those interested in obtaining the franchise to submit their proposals to the council. Eventually the deadline was extended to the end of October, in part because the one company that everyone knew was interested in the franchise, Irving's S.M.T. (Eastern) Limited, had not submitted a proposal. The reason it had not done so was the secret agreement that Irving had negotiated – or thought he had – with C.H. Nichols, president of Federal Light and Traction. Mindful of the skirmishing that had developed over the issue a few years before, Irving reasoned that it would be a relatively simple decision for the common council to permit the Power Company to retain the franchise it already had and merely permit it to replace its trams with buses. And since, as a result of the private negotiations, the Power Company had agreed to then sell its expanded franchise to Irving, S.M.T. (Eastern) Limited would operate Saint John's transportation system. It was a simple solution and guaranteed to deliver the franchise to Irving with minimal difficulties. In mid-October, Irving again travelled to New York to confirm the agreement he had originally concluded more than two years before with the president of Federal Light and Traction. And so the revised deadline passed without a proposal from S.M.T. (Eastern) Limited.

But with all the proposals in, the Power Company refused to sell the street railway system and the franchise for the price agreed upon. No doubt seizing the opportunity for a quick gain the Power Company had put Irving in a difficult spot: if he refused to meet the increased price, it might well be forty years before another opportunity to acquire the system came up. And because greatly increased wartime demands in the port city had dangerously overburdened the street railway system, the councillors were so eager to get buses to replace the trams that they offered to guarantee the Power Company against losses if it would order a fleet of buses: it was a seller's market.

Irving continued to negotiate the Power Company's increased price for the franchise. The negotiations continued through the holidays and throughout January, but no agreement was reached. Finally, on February 9, 1942, Irving increased his offer to an amount he was pretty sure would be acceptable to the Power Company. Irving thought the franchise was his. At the very least, he figured, the Power Company had agreed to give him the opportunity to purchase the transportation system at any figure that any other prospective purchaser might offer for it.

But exactly one week later, on March 16, R.W. Harris, vice-president of United Services Corporation, announced that F.C. Manning had purchased the Power Company's transportation system for an undisclosed price, rumoured to be about $150,000. His company, he said, would take possession immediately and would have buses on the streets within the week. Two days later four of Manning's brand new blue and white buses were carrying passengers throughout the city, with more promised in a few days.

Irving, no doubt, was dumbfounded. Manning had spectacularly outmanoeuvred him once again. There was only one recourse. The day after the announcement Irving was in court applying for an injunction to restrain the Power Company from completing the proposed transfer to the United Services Corporation. Irving submitted an affidavit in support of the injunction application, outlining the history of the negotiations he had had with the Power Company and claiming that the company had failed to honour the agreement made (though not actually signed) between them. Chief Justice J.B.M. Baxter granted the injunction until March 30. But, following the hearing of the injunction suit on March 28, the Chief Justice stated that unless he could see a contract in written form he would be constrained to dissolve the injunction, which he thereupon did. The sale could then be completed.

But perhaps anticipating such a decision and worried that Manning's company might not preserve certain rights the city enjoyed with the Power Company, the city appealed to the provincial attorney-general to seek an injunction on its behalf. The same morning he dissolved the S.M.T. injunction, Chief Justice Baxter granted a temporary injunction to the city restraining the transfer for thirty days. Mayor C.R. Wasson was remarkably quiet about the city's injunction suit. Other than declaring it was to protect the city's rights, he said nothing.

Apparently thinking – as most other people did – that the city objected to the sale itself, two days after the injunction was granted Irving submitted a proposal for an exclusive franchise to common council. It seemed like an ideal opportunity and Irving's franchise proposal was most generous – so generous that it looks as though by this time winning meant more to him than making a profitable deal. He proposed that the city determine the routes, the fares, schedules and times, that a councillor sit on the company's board of directors and that the company would pay the city taxes or fifty percent of the profits of the company, whichever was greater. He also wrote to the councillors that in anticipation of getting the franchise he had on February 25 ordered ten new buses from the Ford Motor Company, specially designed for civic transit. Common council discussed the proposal with a notable lack of enthusiasm. Two weeks later Irving sent council a letter in support of his application. He wrote that "past experience with outside control of the city's transportation system has not been satisfactory – local ownership and direction by a substantial local industry, in co-operation with the city, would be far more beneficial from every standpoint." He noted that last year his companies – which had, as he often said, "chosen" to establish their head office in Saint John – employed 655 people, had a payroll of $716,078.50 and paid out $28,293.30 in taxes. The city was unmoved. In fact, the same day the council discussed Irving's second letter, W.P. Southard, vice-president and general manager of the Power Company, announced that the sale of his company's transportation system to United Services Corporation and F.C. Manning had been completed. That morning the city and the two companies had signed an agreement granting the city the same privileges it enjoyed with the Power Company, but "in more definite and extensive terms," commented the mayor. Later that day the parties met Chief Justice Baxter in his chambers in Saint John and requested that he dissolve the interim injunction. The sale was complete and Manning's buses were back on the street. Not to be outdone by Irving, Manning announced that his company had ordered twenty new buses from the Ford Motor Company and was expecting delivery shortly.

Manning had overcome Irving's best efforts to block the sale, but the fight wasn't over yet. Ten days later, on April 28, the provincial attorney-general, at the relation of seven Saint John ratepayers, commenced the third injunction application. The seven ratepayers were led by Ralph G. McInerney, an insurance agent (who, incidentally, wrote most of the insurance for S.M.T.) and represented by the ubiquitous Cyrus F. Inches. They claimed that the sale was null and void because neither company had the power or authority to enter into such an agreement. Chief Justice Baxter granted the injunction prohibiting the transfer and issued a mandatory injunction requiring the Power Company to continue operating the street railway system. Manning's buses were off the streets again. Before the issue could come to trial, the Wartime Federal Transit Controller visited the city and ordered the Power Company to continue operating the system until the question was resolved by the provincial legislature. Manning's rights were transferred back to the Power Company.

It was a victory of sorts. The injunction prevented the system's transfer to Manning, but just as surely it prevented its transfer to Irving. The next sitting of the legislature was in the spring of 1943, more than a year away. Meanwhile the Power Company continued its modest track improvement program and pressed the transit controller to obtain a few more buses to augment the street railway system. Overall, the system deteriorated still further. It was the citizens of Saint John who had lost.

The next spring a bill to confirm the sale was introduced in the legislature by Saint John Conservative M.L.A. W. Grant Smith. Since the bill was no more than the agreement signed by the parties last April, routine passage was expected. In fact it produced a series of the most stormy and confusing sessions the Corporations Committee of the legislature had seen.

The city, perhaps wiser as a result of the string of franchise applications from S.M.T. over the past year, began by asking for three amendments to the original bill. In the first and most contentious amendment the city stated that it wanted nothing in the agreement to give the company any right to run buses in the city. The city stated that it had never given anyone the right to run buses and only suffered the Power Company to do so as an extension of the street railway system. The city's lawyer, E.J. Henneberry, argued repeatedly that there had never been a question of any bus franchise in transactions connected with the sale of the street railway to Manning's company. "In fact," he said, "Mr. Manning himself at the time stated he had not been granted a bus franchise." P.J. Hughes, acting for both the Power Company and Transportation Corporation, strenuously objected. The city had made an agreement, he charged, and then sought to have it changed by the legislature. "Now they are asking that no bus franchise be granted. This is ridiculous." His clients, he said, would not accept this change. "The amendments are a case of trying to get a new right and we cannot agree to them." Clearly, it was one thing for Manning to comfort the city by saying he wasn't asking for a bus franchise while at the same time announcing that he was planning to replace the trams and had ordered twenty buses; and entirely another for the city to say he didn't have a bus franchise at all. One way, he all but had a bus franchise and could work out the details with the city at his convenience; the other way, he had purchased a street railway system that was worth little more than its value as scrap.

The confusing debate raged for two days. In addition to the original bill, each side introduced their own amended versions. Legislators, lawyers, interested parties and spectators so crowded the hearings room that the Corporations Committee was forced to adjourn to the more spacious legislative chamber itself – not the last time a case involving Irving would pull a committee out into the open spaces of the Assembly Chamber. After two days of public debate, private sessions and innumerable compromise attempts, the parties still could not reach agreement. Cyrus F. Inches, counsel for S.M.T., , was one of the last speakers before the committee. For an hour and a half,

Inches traced the history of Irving's struggle to acquire the transportation franchise. Bringing the history to date, Inches said that he was "astounded" to read in the press one morning the previous spring that the common council had signed an agreement and that a deed of transfer from the Power Company to United Services Corporation had also been signed. "Recently the Common Council said if they don't go ahead the citizens will accuse them of keeping outside capital from the city – that the city will get the reputation of being a closed corporation. Where will the profits go, to the residents of the City of Halifax?" Arguing from what was rapidly becoming the standard Irving position, Inches went on, "The mayor now has a chance to keep in Saint John a large New Brunswick company centred in Saint John – S.M.T. When we have such a large industry in Saint John, employing many people, paying large amounts in taxes and wages, then the attitude the city adopts is one of unconcern. Is there no protection for industries in New Brunswick?" Turning to Hughes, he declared that "the cat was out of the bag at last." "Under the interpretation Mr. Manning and his solicitors put on the different acts granting a franchise to run a street railway," he said, "there was given also a franchise to run buses. Then the city found that the Manning interests thought they were buying the perpetual rights to run a bus system and the city submitted an amendment." He concluded by saying that he thought that the committee would agree that this entire matter should be deferred until the end of the war.

Neither the city nor the Transportation Corporation agreed that the issue should be postponed; but since no agreement seemed possible, the bill confirming the sale was withdrawn. No one knew what that would mean to the city's transportation system, or what the next move would be. But they didn't have to wait long to find out. Three weeks after the bill was withdrawn, Manning startled the city by announcing that he had purchased a controlling interest in the New Brunswick Power Company. It was the obvious solution. Since it had proved impossible to get a favourable bill through the legislature authorizing transfer of the transportation system, Manning reasoned that if he bought the whole Power Company there would be no need to transfer the transportation system to Transportation Corporation and thus no need for legislative approval.

It was a remarkable coup. At one stroke he had removed the city to the weaker bargaining position and all but forced Irving out of the contest. Manning no longer had to bargain with the city to get a bill passed in the legislature: the purchase of the transportation system alone was subject to legislative approval – but not that of the whole kit and caboodle. Moreover, since the Power Company had a perpetual franchise – although not an exclusive one – to operate at least a street railway in the city, and since the Federal Transit Controller had ruled that he would not permit a dual transportation system in Saint John, even if the city awarded a franchise to Irving he would be effectively prohibited from exercising it at least until the end of the war. If the city wanted buses, Manning would have to run them.

Lest the common councillors had any illusions about their position, Manning explained it to them that fall. In late October 1943, Manning told the councillors that before his company proceeded with any capital expenditures on the transportation system it wanted a definite franchise agreement. "It was impossible," he emphasized "for the Power Company to do anything to improve the transportation system in Saint John until the whole transportation question had been settled and some definite agreement reached." He suggested that a franchise agreement for "the term of fifteen years would be adequate". The only alternative was for his company to take the buses off the streets and attempt to improve the street railway system. The war had placed an almost intolerable burden on the system as it was; without buses to augment the trains, the whole system would collapse.

Maritime Transit Controller Albert C. Wagner (the man who, six months earlier, before the legislature Corporations Committee, Cyrus F. Inches had called "an employee of Mr.

Manning") appeared before council and in effect strengthened Manning's case. He revealed that the Federal Transit Controller had alloted nine buses to Saint John with delivery expected in December. "The New Brunswick Power Company has ordered them," he said, "and to the best of my knowledge, will get them." But he added that they had not yet been paid for. There was no doubt that the city needed the buses. But the clear implication was that if the Power Company didn't operate them – and to do that it wanted a franchise – the city wouldn't get them. Moreover, he repeatedly emphasized that his office would prohibit a dual transportation system in the city. Mayor Wasson commented that the general feeling was that the street railway was finished and that it should be scrapped. Manning replied that to scrap it would cost millions of dollars and take twenty-five years. Clearly Manning was not eager to abandon the system until he had a bus franchise. As long as he retained the system he had a perpetual franchise to operate it and since the transit controller prohibited dual systems, only the Power Company could operate buses.

The logic was unassailable. The next day Irving, accompanied by S.M.T. officers W.W. Rogers and T. Bell, along with solicitors Cyrus Inches and Louis Ritchie, appeared before council to argue the Irving case. For the council to be contemplating making a franchise proposal to the Power Company, he said, was unfair to S.M.T., which had had its application on file with the council since March of 1942. "You have our proposition," he continued. "As citizens of Saint John we are entitled to preferential treatment, and we want the franchise." The S.M.T. argument hinged on Ritchie's statement that the Federal Transit Controller had told him that a dual transportation system in Saint John was "inadvisable", but not prohibited. It was a weak argument and within a few days Mayor Wasson received confirmation from the transit controller that a dual system was indeed prohibited. At the same time, the mayor declared that council would take no further action on the franchise proposal until the end of the war. Irving was not unhappy with the decision. He had repeatedly urged council to table the matter until war's end simply because under the order prohibiting dual systems S.M.T. was unlikely to be allotted buses.

But the Power Company refused to allow the common council to bury its collective head. Nor for that matter was the council willing to abandon the issue unresolved. A month and a half later, five days after Christmas 1943, acting on Mayor Wasson's suggestion, and faced with a 7,000 signature petition demanding a solution to the problem, the council passed a resolution offering the Power Company a five-year franchise. "My suggestion," said the Mayor, "is prompted only by a desire to be fair to a corporation who are now by circumstances beyond our control serving our people, and at the same time make a sincere gesture to encourage the best possible bus and street car transportation for our citizens." A week later, following a letter from S.M.T., the council decided to throw the whole issue into the open again and set up a special two-man commission charged with drawing up a model franchise agreement.

For the next nine months the two commissioners – J.F.H. Teed, a Saint John solicitor, and deGaspe Beaubien, a Montreal consulting engineer – studied the franchise problem and discussed it with representatives of S.M.T. and the Power Company. Then on September 15, 1944, acting on the recommendations of the commission, common council and representatives of the neighbouring parishes of Lancaster and Simonds agreed to offer a five-year bus franchise to the Power Company. Before the end of the month the agreement was signed by Mayor Wasson and F.C. Manning. Although it still needed legislative approval, the mayor and councillors congratulated themselves on finally making a firm decision. Manning was pleased but subdued, no doubt recalling the difficulties a similar bill encountered in the legislature the past spring. Irving was ominously quiet.

That winter – the worst, it was said, in ten years – the city's transportation system came close to collapse. On November 24, a Canadian Pacific freighter grounding on a reef in the harbour curtailed operations of the cross-harbour ferry and greatly increased the load on the city's street cars. To compound the problem, frequent heavy snow storms and high winds caused power interruptions that brought the electric trams to a halt. Because the franchise agreement still lacked final approval, Manning declined to press the transit controller for more buses. And citizens of the port city trudged to work through the snow, and complained.

It was clear that everyone expected the city's transportation bill to be the most controversial bill before the legislature that spring. When the bill finally came up for debate in the Municipalities Committee on March 23, 1945, the expectations were not disappointed. To the common council and supporters of the Power Company, the winter's near disaster only proved the necessity of quick passage for the bill. To those who disapproved of the bill – chiefly S.M.T. – the difficulties demonstrated once again that the Power Company was incapable of operating a good transportation system.

The debate on the bill before the Municipalities Committee raged from early morning until late that night when the bill was referred to private session of the committee. Mayor James D. McKenna (elected that fall), J.F.H. Teed and eight other speakers appeared in the morning to urge the committee to approve the bill. "I am here to endorse the action of the previous Common Council," said Mayor McKenna, "and to ask that this bill be approved. Possibly never in the history of Saint John has there been such a breakdown in the transportation of the city as there was this winter. Labour suffered great disadvantages in getting to and from work. It was necessary to use trucks in some cases to get the men to the West Side. I don't hesitate to say this – I hope Saint John will never be confronted again with the chaos we had this winter. . . . I am supporting this bill because a contract was entered into with the Power Company, and also in light of my experiences during the last winter."

The only speaker during the afternoon sitting was Cyrus F. Inches, representing S.M.T., who opposed the bill. Inches began – as he always did – with a lengthy history outlining Irving's attempt to get the city's bus franchise. He concluded the history by giving the committee a document entitled "Comparison of Costs", prepared by private consultants and auditors hired by S.M.T. which purported to show that the cost to the city, if it awarded the franchise to the Power Company, would be $868,235 more than if it was awarded to S.M.T. The charges were a surprise to those advocating the bill and were – at least in the public sessions – never adequately answered. Inches argued persuasively that the S.M.T. franchise proposal would be far more beneficial to the city than the agreement it already had with the Power Company. Teed responded that "both Mr. Irving and Mr. Manning had tried to get the Power Company. Mr. Manning got it – that was just too bad for Mr. Irving," he continued. "If he had got control, he would be here today seeking approval of such a bill as this rather than opposing it."

Inches mounted an organized, articulate and well-documented opposition against the disarrayed proponents of the bill. Committee chairman J.K. McKee, a Liberal M.L.A. from Liberal Irving's Kent County, apparently agreed with Inches that the bill was not in the city's best interest and after several private sessions over the next few weeks, the committee turned it down.

Clearly, Irving was learning how to use the government. Although he was the only opposing voice, he had frustrated the wishes of the common council, the Power Company, the Saint John Port Workers, the Saint John Marine and Shipbuilding Workers and probably most of the citizens. But Irving had won, or at least he had prevented the Power Company from winning. Of course there were mutterings that politics were involved in the committee's decision, but they rarely came into the open and when they did Irving denied them.

Nothing had changed. The Power Company wasn't about to order more buses or tear up the street railway until it had the financial security a franchise would provide. It still had a franchise agreement with the city, but that was of little value unless it could get legislative approval and it couldn't do that

77

until the next spring. Even S.M.T. couldn't realistically negotiate for a franchise as long as the Federal Transit Controller had authority. Certainly, it was said, S.M.T. wouldn't be allotted buses to run in the city. Now it was Irving who was beginning to look like a dog in a manger. Then on July 15, 1945, the federal government announced that the Federal Transit Control office was closed and all restrictions removed. It was a whole new ball game.

Common council didn't lose any time. The next day, after three hours of often heated debate, the councillors resolved to enter into a six-year agreement with the Power Company. The agreement – the councillors were careful not to call it a franchise, although the city promised not to operate during the six years – would require the company to buy twelve new buses and convert the city's transportation system as rapidly as possible from street cars to buses. The vote was four to two with Mayor McKenna and one councillor opposing the resolution. The mayor complained that S.M.T. should at least be given a hearing. It was his firm belief, he said, that any franchise which would be awarded should "be in the best interests of the citizens . . . and the only way of doing that is to permit the firms concerned to make an offer to the council." Councillor Kennedy agreed. Referring to the franchise bill defeated in the legislature that spring, he noted, "some have said that the opposition company has been instrumental in having it defeated. This sort of talk was most unjust." He pointed out that now, however, the city was in the best position to get the best bargain. "The fact that there has been no advance notice of the action to be taken by the council was vastly unfair," he said. Nevertheless, the majority of councillors were tired of waiting and wanted action. The Power Company, they thought, offered a reasonable deal. City solicitor J.F.H. Teed agreed. The agreement was signed and the Power Company ordered the twelve new buses.

But before the councillors could draw breath to heave a sigh of relief, Irving was in court applying for an injunction. The agreement was signed Monday and on Wednesday Louis

Ritchie appeared before Justice Harrison of the provincial Supreme Court, seeking an interim injunction on behalf of S.M.T. (Eastern) Limited "and all other ratepayers and inhabitants of the City of Saint John", restraining the city from executing the agreement it had made with the Power Company. Ritchie claimed that the agreement was illegal and *ultra vires* because, among other reasons, the company did not have a licence from the Motor Carrier Board to operate buses and the city hadn't received the approval of the legislature. Justice Harrison granted the injunction. The city then attempted to parry Irving's thrust. On the advice of city solicitor J.F.H. Teed, common council passed a resolution authorizing the Power Company to operate buses in the city and amended a 1921 bylaw to similar effect. The purpose, Teed argued, was to clear up any legal doubts as to the authority of the Power Company to operate buses in Saint John. The resolutions again passed by a four to two vote with McKenna and Kennedy opposed. The mayor declared that he had received legal advice to take no part in the deliberations until it was clearly indicated that they were not in contempt of court. Councillor Kennedy thought the people would get a better bargain from S.M.T. But the general feeling of council seemed to be summed up by Councillor Wasson, the former mayor: "We want adequate transportation and we want it now." Moreover, the councillors' determination to complete the agreement with the Power Company seemed, if anything, to be heightened by Irving's opposition. "We are trying to do something for the citizens," complained one councillor, "but are always being blocked. We must have the courage of our convictions."

And they needed it. Two days later, before the injunction suit had come to trial, action was commenced by the provincial attorney-general at the relation of S.M.T. (Eastern) Limited against the city, the surrounding parishes of Lancaster and Simonds and the Power Company, claiming that the agreement signed by the city and the company was illegal and ultra vires. But before the end of the year, Justice Harrison dismissed the injunction suit and the two parties agreed to use the same affidavits in the suit brought by the Attorney-General *ex relatione* S.M.T. (Eastern) Limited. Argument in that suit before Justice P.J. Hughes, the former Power Company solicitor who had recently been appointed to the bench, continued sporadically for almost two years. Finally, on September 11, 1947, Justice Hughes dismissed the case with costs. "The intention of the parties to the conflict," declared the Justice, "was to benefit the public. In making provision for new buses to replace the old electrically-drawn street cars they were making satisfactory arrangements. It would be unfortunate if the court had to interfere to prevent this arrangement being put into effect."

And that was that. Or almost; three months later, on December 11, 1947, S.M.T. appealed the case, but it was again dismissed.

Meanwhile, the Power Company was in trouble. Aside from the demoralizing effect of repeated injunctions, the company still lacked a long term agreement with the city and consequently was reluctant to invest very heavily in the city's transportation system. Immediate post-war supply problems had delayed the company's plans still further. Delivery of the twelve trolley buses the company had ordered from Canadian Car and Foundry in Fort William was first scheduled for December 1945, then April 1946, then August, then April 1947, and finally September. But when the buses arrived the company found it couldn't get some of the parts necessary to install the overhead wiring. More delays.

Finally, in mid-September, Mayor McKenna requested a meeting with Power Company officials to discuss the problem. The company said that since it couldn't get the equipment needed for trolley buses, it would try to order gasoline buses. Mayor McKenna suggested that a franchise agreement might speed removal of the tram system and the Power Company agreed. The same day S.M.T. filed notice that it would appeal Justice Hughes' ruling in the injunction suit. And Saint John commuters looked forward to a long cold winter.

A month later, with the situation depressingly the same and

no new buses in sight, the city attempted to resolve the problem. Mayor McKenna moved that the city approach the legislature in the spring for authority to purchase the Power Company's assets, including the transportation system. If the legislature approved the plebiscite on public ownership, and if the citizens voted for it, said the mayor, the city would exercise its option and enter final negotiations with the Power Company. The councillors agreed. Meanwhile, Mayor McKenna told Manning that the city would not be interested in purchasing its trolley buses. Consequently, said Manning, his company stopped negotiating for them. But while the city was debating the plan, the province acted. On the evening of December 2, in a surprise announcement (at least it was a surprise to Manning), Liberal Premier J.B. McNair said that the provincial government had expropriated the Power Company's generating and distribution systems, for a rumoured $3,000,000. "It was hoped by the expropriation," said the premier, "to overcome a serious power shortage and avoid the necessity of rigid rationing." The premier revealed that one of the province's electric generators would have to be shut down for repairs and another because of low water levels – and that the Power Company had a surplus.

The Power Company was gutted by expropriation; the substance of the company, and its chief source of revenue, was the power generating and distribution system. And while it may have neglected the transportation system, it certainly had taken care of the generating facilities. Two and a half years before, the company had ordered $1,250,000 worth of new generating equipment, which had recently been installed – all of which was now the property of the provincial government; a Liberal government which Manning must have suspected of collusion with the prominent Kent County Liberal, K.C. Irving. And Manning's troubles were far from over. At the end of January 1948, the company's car barns burned to the ground in a spectacular fire that destroyed nine buses and caused several hundred thousand dollars in damage. The fire turned the city's transportation crisis to an emergency –

in which common council, surprisingly, moved quickly. On a resolution moved by the former mayor, C.R. Wasson, the council agreed to seek authority at the next session of the provincial legislature to terminate the Power Company's rights to operate a transportation system. The councillors complained that the company had failed to modernize its equipment sufficiently to give even adequate service and that it had failed to scrap the tram system as soon as reasonably possible. In other words, said the council, the company had failed to fulfil its obligations under the agreement signed with the city in the summer of 1945.

Manning was requested to appear before council a few days later to explain his company's position. He seemed tired and defeated, almost bitter. He said he felt the system was reasonably good before the fire, adding that it had been consistently improved since he had taken over the company in 1943. The present winter had been particularly difficult, he said, with snow, storms and abnormally cold weather. "But the main reason the system has not been improved," he said with some petulance, "is that every time we go to make a major move we are blocked by S.M.T. (Eastern) Limited. The city of Saint John is suffering today because of injunctions put on by S.M.T." He explained that building a transportation system required an expenditure of approximately $2,000,000. "Can you reasonably expect any company to undertake such a big operation when it doesn't know from one day to the next whether it will be in business?" he asked. The Power Company had spent money to improve its systems, he told the councillors. Since he took over the management, the company had spent $1,700,000 on improvements. "We spent $1,250,000 for improvements to the generating and distribution system of the company. But within a few days of the completion of this expenditure, the generation and distribution system was expropriated by the New Brunswick Electric Power Commission." At the present time, he said, his company was reluctant to go ahead with large capital expenditures for new equipment in view of the city's action last week in seeking authority from the legislature to terminate the Power Company's privileges in the city. Asked by another councillor how quickly he could improve the situation if all obstacles were removed, Manning said there wasn't much hope of that; that there probably would be further litigation.

At its next meeting two days later, council received representatives of both the Power Company and S.M.T. F.M. Sutherland, vice-president and general manager of the Power Company, said that he was sure his company could get ten buses from Canadian Car and Foundry in Fort William within eight days after ordering, allowing four days for delivery. The whole shipment, he said, would arrive in eighteen days. He understood that there were more buses available in the Maritimes, but he could only think of one. The council then asked W.W. Rogers, president of S.M.T., where his company stood. Well, said Mr. Rogers, S.M.T. was definitely interested in local operations. And it just happened to have seventeen city transit type buses in storage at Pennfield, just outside the city, that could be put in operation immediately. These could be supplemented, he added, from the 130 buses the company operated throughout the province, some on a seasonal basis. It was a masterful stroke.

"If S.M.T. were public-spirited," said one councillor, "they would offer to lend their buses to the Power Company in this emergency." At that point Louis Ritchie jumped up. It was not fair, he said, "to ask S.M.T. to offer to their competitors equipment to bail them out of a hole when they failed to meet their obligations." In fact, he said, quite the opposite was true. S.M.T. was ready to take over the Power Company's equipment and operate it in the city. Rogers added that his company "did not want to play dog in the manger, but the buses were bought for our own purposes."

Unless the city dropped its applications to the legislature, said the Power Company, it would cancel its order for the ten buses. The city refused to drop it and the Power Company cancelled its order. S.M.T. immediately offered to put its seventeen new buses – presently in storage – and twenty used buses in service in the city as soon as it received the city's permission. The company said it planned to order an additional thirty-one buses immediately. A few weeks later the Power Company announced that it had purchased fifteen used buses from the Toronto Transit Commission and expected them to arrive that morning. But it was too late; the legislature had passed the city's transportation bill on May 1, with little opposition. The bill authorized the city to cancel the Power Company's right to operate in the city at any time within the next six months after seventy-five days notice. The day the bill passed the legislature, the city voted to notify the Power Company. The same day it voted to grant S.M.T. a thirteen-year exclusive franchise to operate buses in the city with a provision for a ten-year renewal when that expired. On July 1, S.M.T. could begin operations in the city.

Both motions passed by a one-vote majority. Councillor Jamieson thought they were "completely unfair, unreasonable and unjust." Moreover, he argued, the council would be committing the city to something which might involve it in a long legal battle. Despite the legislation, the city was still bound by the agreement it had signed with the Power Company in 1945. The agreement could not be terminated unless the council decided that the company had defaulted, but if a board of arbitration concluded that the company had not defaulted the city could be sued by the company for capital loss. But lest the councillors allow that detail to influence their decision to cancel the agreement, S.M.T. said it would protect the city against possible loss resulting from legal action brought by the Power Company.

Councillor Whitebone, representing labour groups in the city, argued that no franchise should be awarded before the October plebiscite on public ownership of the system. Ritchie argued that S.M.T. needed the long-term franchise because of the large investment the company would have to make to establish the service. But finally the company agreed that the city could cancel the franchise on eighteen months notice if the citizens voted in favour of public ownership. But Mayor

McKenna appeared to sum up the feeling of the majority, which seemed to be as much against the Power Company as for S.M.T. "We are either going to improve the transportation system or we are not. We saw a notice published by the New Brunswick Power Company which had the effrontery to say if the city persisted in taking the bill to Fredericton they would order no further buses. . . . After promises not kept, and evasions which we have seen, I am going to support what will give good service this coming winter." Two weeks later, in mid-May, common council met again to consider the S.M.T. proposal to acquire the Power Company's transportation system. Ritchie said that S.M.T. had offered Manning $340,000 for the system, but Manning had refused it. "Mr. Manning said $450,000 would be necessary. S.M.T. in turn offered to pay this sum, but Mr. Manning said an additional $100,000 to $150,000 would be required." Rogers added that his company had learned during the negotiations with the Power Company that had the S.M.T. offer of $450,000 been accepted for the transportation system, the Power Company stood to make a non-taxable capital gain of $1,045,000 through sale of its power system, gas system and transportation system.

"We did not consider the assets worth any more than $325,000," said Irving. "We made the offer under pressure," he added. "Personally, I think it is very bad business to pay the Power Company more than its assets are worth, on top of the handsome profits it has already made through the sale of its electrical facilities." But then that wasn't the city's problem. The council merely sought assurance that those Saint John citizens holding the Power Company bonds would not lose their money. Ritchie assured them that the Power Company's bond holders would be "plentifully reimbursed" if the company lost the transportation system.

After further negotiations, the agreement was concluded and common council satisfied. On the first day of July 1948, Irving's buses appeared on the city's streets, climaxing his twelve-year struggle to get the franchise.

Only one hurdle remained to their continued operation:

the plebiscite on ownership of the transportation system. When the plebiscite came up in October, the citizens voted in favour of public ownership; but six months later, common council – which had clearly had enough – declared that the time was not right to take over operation of the system. Irving's buses have operated in Saint John unhindered ever since. And Fred Manning went back to Halifax to lick his wounds.

Perhaps the most interesting aspect of the whole marathon duel is the comparison between the two major figures. Like Irving, also a Presbyterian, Manning was born in a small town – in his case, Falmouth, Nova Scotia – and learned his business skills early. Like Irving, he began in the automobile business in the twenties, and moved to the business centre of his province in the thirties, expanding into oil. He formed United Services Corporation during the thirties, and expanded into gas stations, transportation, pulp, and so forth. At the time of their confrontation, Manning was almost exactly, in Halifax, what Irving was in Saint John.

It is fascinating to speculate on the contrasts: just as Manning lost the franchise, he lost the long-run competition. He never became for Nova Scotia what Irving became for New Brunswick, and it is clear that the turning point for each of them came during the thirties and forties. The difference between them in this fight seems to be that Irving learned more – at the beginning, he was as naive as it was possible to be in his position; at the end his political savvy clearly outclassed Manning – and that Irving simply stayed one more round. It is hard to believe that Irving, in Manning's position, would simply have thrown in the towel after the expropriation. Once the bell has rung, Irving is simply incapable of quitting, even when it's to his financial disadvantage to win.

And that's the difference. Ten years later, Manning had sold out United Services and Super-Service to Petrofina and was just another wealthy and successful business executive and member of a multiplicity of boards. Maybe he was happier in such a position; Irving would not have been. Unable to quit,

Irving simply kept on growing to become the Irving dinosaur. In a comparable position, he did not sell Irving Oil to Standard Oil of California: he kept fifty-one percent of the refinery and kept Standard out of the parent company altogether. He is not a member of the board of any company he doesn't dominate; preferably, he will not be on a board if he doesn't own the operation lock, stock and barrel. And that's why the name Irving is known across Canada, the name Manning merely to those who pass by the Manning Memorial Chapel at Acadia University.

CHAPTER THREE

Making It – The War Years

If you are a K.C. Irving, there are all sorts of ways of making money during a war without it being said that you profited from the war. To be sure, you can make money during a war in ways that you can't in peacetime, but that's not necessarily profiteering. A war utilizes all of a country's conventional technological skills and resources and many that are not conventional at all. Only during a war, for instance, could a whole industry grow up around the raising of black widow spiders so the silky material from their webs could be used in bomb sights. But usually the profit is to be made in more conventional ways, like owning a foundry or an electronics plant. Or an aircraft factory. Or even a bus line. A bus line doesn't sound like a very profitable place to make money during a war – but, as a spokesman for Irving's S.M.T. (Eastern) Limited once pointed out, public transit traffic increased eighty per cent between 1939 and 1947. And there's not much reason to think, as the war continued and car production dropped off and gasoline rationing increased, that traffic didn't continue its spectacular increase.

But to say that Irving had bought a bus line in order to profit from rationing and increased traffic during the war would be misleading at best. On the other hand, in 1936 even the most dull-witted and imperceptive businessman could see that a major war was all but inevitable. And Irving was neither dull-witted nor imperceptive.

Similarly, it would be misleading to claim that Irving deliberately held wood from his father's land off the market until the impending war inflated the prices. But as it happened, the war did inflate the prices and Irving began selling the wood. Could he manage it, no businessman would do otherwise. Likewise, in 1938 when Irving bought the nearly bankrupt Canada Veneers, no one could have predicted it would become a multi-million dollar company by the end of the war. But then no one could have foreseen that the company would become the major supplier of aircraft veneers for the all-wood Mosquito bomber. Or that the shipyards of New Brunswick, once world-famous for their wooden ships, would produce the thousands of wooden tenders and plywood invasion barges built at Irving Shipyards Limited at Bouctouche. It's unlikely that Irving could have foreseen all this before the war, but just as unlikely that in 1936 he would see the coming war as a reason for not expanding his holdings. As even a poor businessman will tell you, war is good business. And no one has ever said that Irving is a poor businessman.

During the early thirties, Irving was primarily interested in automobiles, automobile parts and petroleum products. So it was hardly surprising that like other garage owners he began operating buses. If anything was surprising, it was that it took so long – but even that delay, as it turned out, made good business sense.

In 1934 the New Brunswick government proudly claimed that the province contained almost 10,000 miles of roads for the pleasure and enjoyment of its citizens, as well as any tourists who might care to venture on a motor tour of the province. What the government didn't say was that most of the roads were little more than dirt tracks. True, the sparing addition of gravel allowed some of them to be termed "improved", and the province could boast exactly thirteen miles of surfaced roads. But none of these could be considered all-weather roads; and in fact none of them were kept open during the winter.

But then in 1934 neither Nova Scotia nor Prince Edward Island kept any roads open during the winter either. Those people who felt it was necessary to travel more then a few hundred yards down the road – and most didn't – usually traveled by train. Even in summer, those adventurous enough to travel by road were prepared for a dusty, kidney-jarring odyssey that might end suddenly at a washout. Nevertheless, New Brunswick had entered the motor age.

Ten years had elapsed since Irving had installed an old glass-topped gas pump in front of his father's store, eight years since he had taken over a Ford dealership in Saint John, two years since he had opened the Golden Ball Garage in the heart of the city. Garages for storing and repairing cars had sprung up in towns across the province and travel to most places was now possible without an extra can of gasoline. It may not have been all that comfortable, or even practical, but motoring had become a popular way to travel. And as more people bought cars, Irving was there to sell them gasoline and oil, tires and parts. He was there to store their cars in the winter and repair them in the summer. And when their cars had taken that last gasp, he was there to sell them a new one.

But while the rich could afford cars, the poor had to settle for motor buses. And motoring had become such a popular way to travel that many people actually preferred bouncing around the province in motor buses to taking the reliable but usually inconvenient trains. Garage owners quickly recognized this, and were not slow to enter the field. By 1934, sixty buses were licensed to operate in the province and a number were operating without licences. For seven years the provincial Motor Carrier Board had tried to regulate fares, schedules and routes with only marginal success. Though buses were expensive to buy, they could be profitable to operate; consequently, any enterprising garage owner who could borrow the money to buy one of the common twelve passenger, open-top sedan buses was prepared to pick up passengers wherever he could find them and charge whatever the traffic would bear. The usual bus was driven by the man who owned it and its cleanliness and state of repair reflected its owner's habits and aptitudes. Moreover, schedules were often of more help to the competition than to the passengers. If one operator announced that he would arrive to pick up passengers at 3.15, one of his competitors was likely to show up at 3.00 and drive off with the passengers. The next day the first operator would arrive at 2.45 and any passengers foolish enough to believe the posted schedule would arrive in time to see a billow of dust several miles down the road.

Competition was fierce. But the bus operators' complaints about unauthorized competition were mild compared to the railways' complaints about buses. The motor carriers offered unfair competition, screamed the railways, particularly when they picked up passengers across the street from railway stations and charged less money to take them over parallel routes. "The railways sell sometimes below cost and sometimes above cost," claimed Bernard Allen, a C.N.R. economist, at a Motor Carrier Board hearing in 1936, "but they maintain a healthy balance. The motor carriers, on the other hand, are selling below cost consistently. This is not according to the proper economic principles of the country and is injurious." It was scarcely an argument. But then the bus operators knew little about economic principles and cared even less. A few got rich; most were happy if they made enough money to pay for their gas and oil, and some were happy anyway. And since he was supplying most of the operators with gasoline and parts, Irving was happy, too.

But by 1936, the bus operators' unbridled competition and economic naiveté had had two profound results. The railways had stopped looking down on motor carriers as crude and noisome upstarts and attempted, if not to force them out of business, at least to slow their growth. And in early 1936 Premier Allison Dysart's Liberal government belatedly passed a strengthened Motor Carrier Board Act to ensure the province's citizens of efficient, clean and punctual service, and – it was hoped – to protect them from mechanically deficient vehicles. The effect of the strengthened regulations was to require expenditures which many of the small operators simply couldn't afford. Their choice became increasingly clear: bankruptcy or amalgamation. For ten years Irving had waited, apparently content to do no more than sell gas, oil and automotive supplies to the squabbling independent operators. Then, as they began to falter in the mid-thirties, he bought them up.

Some operators, like the Northumberland Bus Company, carrying passengers over the short but potentially profitable route between the adjacent North Shore towns of Chatham and Newcastle, found that strenuous competition had left them too poor to afford even the provincial licensing fees. Others, like the Saint John Motor Line Limited, operating local routes in the Saint John area with half-a-dozen buses, found themselves bankrupt when the Irving Oil Company which had so readily extended a long line of credit suddenly reeled it in. The company's directors were forced to sell its assets and franchises to Irving Oil at a bargain basement price. Another discovered that a staggering eighty-two per cent of its annual expenses went to Irving-owned companies and finally sold out to its major creditor. Between 1934 and 1936 the number of licensed buses in the province dropped from sixty to forty-three, while Irving quietly snapped up nine bus companies and two trucking companies, giving him a network of routes stretching around the province. Almost overnight Irving had become the province's largest passenger bus and freight truck operator. Although the bus business generally was in difficult economic straits, Irving, by consolidating routes and improving business practices, was in a good position to compete with the railways – an excellent position, in fact, since he now owned both the bus companies and their suppliers. All that remained was for him to amalgamate his various holdings. In September of 1936, Louis Ritchie appeared before the Motor Carrier Board and, to some surprise and consternation, requested the transfer of the various franchises to the S.M.T. System. The Motor Carrier Board approved the transfers and S.M.T. continued to absorb smaller operators and apply for new franchises.

A year later, S.M.T. ran twenty-three buses in New Brunswick, over half the buses in the province. It operated over most of the major routes, as well as substantial routes in Nova Scotia and Prince Edward Island. In New Brunswick in 1937 the company carried 375,000 passengers over almost 1,000 miles of routes, made a gross profit of $160,000 and used 200,-000 gallons of fuel and lubricants. In 1942 the company operated thirty-four buses in the province, carried 1,225,000 passengers and made a gross profit of $592,750. In five years, then, public transit traffic – and profits – had increased by close to 300 per cent and the war was only half over.

The phenomenal increase can be largely attributed to wartime conditions: restrictions on private automobiles and mobilization of a vast civilian labour force. But Irving wasn't content simply to bask in fortune's favour. Not only did he continue to increase his control of the motor transportation industry in the province, acquiring companies and applying for new routes, he regularly went to court seeking the immediate prosecution of any independent operators who dared to infringe on S.M.T.'s exclusive freight or passenger franchises. Late in 1938, for instance, Louis Ritchie appeared before the provincial Motor Carrier Board to ask that the board prosecute six individuals who, Ritchie claimed, were operating over routes S.M.T. held under franchise. H.A. Carr, chairman of the Motor Carrier Board, replied that the board's usual practice was to give permission to prosecute, but to let those interested undertake the prosecutions themselves and bear the expense. Carr didn't mean, however, that the board was unwilling to assist in obtaining the prosecutions. "We find it hard to get evidence," Ritchie told the board, "if the R.C.M.P. would stop and search the trucks, they could get the evidence, whereas we can't." "You tell me what you want," replied the secretary of the board, "and we'll get it." But as Irving had discovered before, often you don't need to go to court just as long as everyone knows you are prepared to go.

The time was over when the independent operator could haul freight or drive passengers at will over the province's roads. The threat of police searches and court action gave even legitimate operators cause for concern. The trend clearly favoured the large and well-organized over the small and independent operators. And, of course, the only large and well-organized operator in the province was Irving's S.M.T. (Eastern) Limited. As if to confirm the trend, at the same time Ritchie asked for the Motor Carrier Board's help in prosecuting independent operators, Chairman Carr stated the principle on which the board would now issue franchises: "The francises must go to those with the facilities and capabilities to give service such as the public must have." He added, "We cannot give consideration to every Tom, Dick and Harry who has an old car with which he thinks he can handle passengers." The chairman's concern may have been for the comfort and safety of the bus passengers, but the result was to favour the province's largest bus company over any other applicants.

Increasing involvement in the bus transportation system seemed, characteristically, only to whet Irving's appetite for absolute control. Late in 1940, for instance, S.M.T. complained to the Motor Carrier Board that taxis were infringing on its franchise between Fredericton and suburban Devon – a matter of a few city blocks. It is difficult to believe that anyone could take such a case very seriously, but the company turned it over to the provincial attorney-general. Irving companies do not take infringement of their rights lightly.

S.M.T. was a profitable system, doubly so because Irving also owned the companies that supplied it with gasoline, oil and equipment. The largest single expense outside the Irving network of companies was for the buses themselves. This was the only breach in the vertically integrated transportation system, but it was a serious one. As he acquired more and more bus companies in the middle thirties, Irving was quick to realize that he was fast building a captive market for buses of his own manufacture. If he were to build his own buses, he would complete the corporate chain and utilize available facilities and talents that would otherwise be wasted. Besides, there were other bus companies operating in the Maritimes who no doubt would be happy to buy better buses manufactured in the Maritimes for less money. And incidentally, of course, Irving would increase his control over the whole industry. It was an attractive proposition, at least partly because he already had the space in which to build his own buses.

At the height of the Depression, in 1932, Irving had purchased a vacant five-story brick building at the corner of Sydney and Union Streets in downtown Saint John to house his growing Ford dealership (since 1931 known as Universal Sales Limited). The "Golden Ball Building" – so called because of two-foot bronzed metal sphere which had been suspended from its corner since the nineteenth century – was just a block down Union Street from his old building, but it was a much better location. Best of all, there was plenty of room for expansion. Space was made on one corner of the ground floor for gas pumps and much of the rest of the floor was used for displaying automobiles and parts. While part of the upper floors of the former department store were used for offices and automobile storage and repair, most of the building remained empty. So, in February of 1936, when Irving was acquiring his own market for buses, it was easy enough to expand the existing auto body repair shop in one corner of the third floor into a small manufacturing facility. The shop had hand fabricated a few vehicle bodies before the expansion, though it didn't have adequate machinery to turn them out on a production basis. But, by early spring, the manufacturing equipment was installed and Universal Sales Limited, Manufacturing Division, was in full operation, employing twelve people to produce bus bodies. The division expanded rapidly, hiring an additional twenty-three people by the end of the summer. In its first five months of production the division produced six bus bodies to be mounted on the imported British Leyland chassis, manufacturing them on the third floor and assembling them on the second. By fall, ten more bodies were under construction and another four ordered. A company official said that "replacements which a number of Maritime bus lines are contemplating, quite apart from any orders for new services, assures the maintenance of the plant's activity at the present pace at least."

But, as Irving continued to create and expand his own market, the plant expanded apace. The next year the operation was moved to larger rented quarters in a part of the old Cornwall Cotton Mill building on Wall Street (which was purchased by Irving two years later to house Canada Veneers). Even that space seemed too small by the end of 1937 and Wendell W. Rogers, S.M.T. manager, announced that the company was planning a further expansion of the body-manufacturing plant, control of which had now been transferred to the bus company, and was seeking larger premises. "The new building would house our body building plant and at the same time provide a central repair depot for the S.M.T. bus fleet," said Rogers. "The enlarged facilities contemplated would enable the company to build truck bodies which are now imported from Ontario. So far we have not built standard bodies but only special types." The plant did expand – and expand again – over the next couple of years, but the war intervened to curtail production severely. Some buses were produced during the war, but by war's end production had stopped. Materials were hard to get and as some of the big aircraft plants turned to bus production, it was cheaper to buy than manufacture your own.

(That, however, wasn't to be the last time Irving built buses. In 1968, over thirty years later, he began manufacturing buses again. This time it was school buses in a converted saw mill, under the trade name Atlantic Bus. Once again he had seen a ready market and quickly stepped in to take advantage of it. This time the market for buses was provided by the sweeping school consolidations under the Robichaud government's Equal Opportunity program. Dozens of one-room country schools were closed and students were taken by bus to larger schools in cities and towns. In its first year Atlantic Truck and Trailer Limited sold eighty-one buses, all of them in New Brunswick. The plant, said the then Liberal Economic Growth Minister, Robert Higgins, was the first outside of Ontario to take advantage of the Canada-United States Auto Pact, allowing for duty free imports of parts. And Irving still builds buses.)

Once in the business of selling gasoline and oil, it was logical that Irving would expand by selling and manufacturing the vehicles that use those products. In fact, from the time he installed that first gasoline pump in Boutouche, all of his business activities revolved around oil. He installed more gasoline pumps, built gasoline stations and repair and storage garages, assembled bus and freight trucking lines and facilities for manufacturing the vehicles those companies used, sold automotive parts and bought ships and tanks for transporting and storing his oil. It was the oil business that Irving knew best and the oil business that he devoted his time and energy to developing. Though Irving's father, like most other large and successful New Brunswick businessmen at the turn of the century, was primarily a lumberman, and though it may have been the lumber business that young Kenneth Irving grew up with, it was not the business he was interested in.

In 1933, J.D. Irving died at the age of seventy-three. K.C. Irving took control of his father's store, his sawmill and his seven thousand acres of woodland. In the early years of the Depression, J.D. Irving Limited was a relatively small company, turning out about two million feet of long lumber a year. "It was just a small company – not big enough to be unwieldy," Irving has recalled, "just big enough to show me how the lumber business operated – to get my foot in the door." Though in 1933 it was clear that Irving's main interest wasn't in wood, ironically it was the lumber business that proved to be Irving's most successful wartime business venture. Perhaps even more ironically, it wasn't his father's lumber business that was so phenomenally successful but rather Canada Veneers, a company he acquired – at least in part – as an addition to his fledgling oil and transportation empire.

A veneer plywood plant seems an improbable addition to that empire until you realize that, in addition to its usual uses in furniture and appliances, hardwood veneer plywood was used extensively in the manufacture of buses. Consequently, when the owners of the small veneer plant sought Irving's help following a disastrous fire and persistent operating difficulties, no doubt it looked like an investment that would both enhance his growing bus-manufacturing division and ensure a continuing supply of local veneers. But within a few years the demand for veneer plywood in the construction of buses had become negligible, replaced by the tremendous wartime demand for aircraft veneers. And Canada Veneers grew from a small and nearly bankrupt provincial operation to the largest supplier of hardwood veneers in the world. But Irving couldn't have foreseen that development when he invested in the company in 1938, any more than Fred Roderick could have foreseen it when he opened the factory on the outskirts of Saint John five years earlier.

The converted grandstand at the Coldbrook Park trotting oval on the Marsh Road was scarcely an ideal building for a veneer mill. But when Roderick, president of the Wilson Box and Lumber Company, incorporated Canada Veneers early in 1933 it was the only large building he could find at his price, with surrounding land for log storage, in all of Saint John. The race track, built in 1930, had been used on only a few occasions for its original purpose in the three years before Canada Veneers moved into the three-story wooden grandstand. Although the country was still in the depths of the Depression, there was a small and developing market for veneer woods used in cheap furniture. Though undercapitalized and financially weak, the company grew slowly and steadily until by the first months of 1936 it employed sixty men on two shifts. As long as the national economy continued its slow upward swing, it seemed that the company would survive, perhaps prosper.

Then, on a mid-March evening in 1936, a fire of mysterious origin burned the converted wooden building to the ground and with it the company's production of veneer wood and its supply of logs. It was a spectacularly disastrous fire. Thousands of people from Saint John were drawn to the scene by the glare in the night sky. "For a time," reported the Saint John *Evening Times-Globe*, "motorists approached the scene four abreast on the Rothesay Road, which was practically impassable for vehicles proceeding toward Saint John." By the time the Saint John Fire Department reached the scene all that remained standing was a skeleton of wooden beams, which, still afire, fell to the ground and sent showers of sparks and burning fragments about the district to ignite small piles of lumber and outlying sheds. Company officials estimated their loss at $150,000, only a part of which was covered by insurance.

Despite this severe loss, the company purchased the old brick Cornwall Cotton Mill on Wall Street at the beginning of July and announced that it had ordered new machinery and would resume production that October, employing about the same number of men as it had before the fire. The company purchased the vacant sixty-year-old mill property – a city block of twelve buildings, including various sheds and shops – for $10,000, $30,000 less than was asked for and over $100,-000 less than the assessed value. It was a breathtaking bargain. A few years before, the building itself had been assessed at close to $300,000, and even the land on which it was built, in the valley district of the city, was easily worth the $10,000 paid for both the land and buildings. Nevertheless, faced with the possibility of another sixty men on its welfare rolls, the city went even further, agreeing to exempt the company from taxes for its first year in the building and fix the assessment at $5,000 for the next ten years. Even with the benefit of these almost unbelievably generous concessions, however, the company suffered continuing financial difficulties. The domestic market for hardwood veneers did not grow as rapidly as expected and foreign markets failed to develop. The fire loss had left the company even more disastrously short of capital than it had been, and persistent operating difficulties continued to impair its financial position.

Using only two floors of the four-story building, the company staggered on for nearly two years, making small shipments of veneers to Britain and the United States, but selling most of its production in the Maritimes. By 1938 it teetered on the verge of bankruptcy. Finally, the directors asked Irving – one of the largest local purchasers of veneer wood – if he would provide the necessary capital to rejuvenate the company and assume control. If he was not able to foresee all of Canada Veneers' potential, Irving could certainly see how neatly it fitted the pattern of his evolving corporate structure. He was only too glad to help out, and, as usual, his embrace was permanent and his help overwhelming. He reorganized the management and operating methods at the plant and installed new and up-to-date machinery for high-speed hardwood veneer production. But, most important, he found in Britain a rich market for the company's product.

For years the company had made small shipments of hardwood veneers to Britain, but it had failed to develop a substantial market for its product. Shortly after Irving assumed control, the company began to experiment in cutting aircraft veneer. British aircraft designers were studying the feasibility of using the light, strong wood in aircraft construction in place of increasingly scarce aluminum. Anticipating a growing shortage of aircraft metals, the British government encouraged their study and shortly issued a specification for aircraft quality hardwood veneer. In early May 1939, Canada Veneers sent a shipment of its new product to Britain: it was approved by both the manufacturers and the government. Substantial orders quickly followed.

But what Irving probably didn't know, even when he directed the company to meet the British government's specifications, were the top secret plans for an all-wood, high-speed bomber. At almost the same time Irving assumed control of the bankrupt Canada Veneers, a small design team at the DeHavilland Aircraft Company was conceiving plans for a light bomber which was to rely for its safety on speed rather than armament, and was to be built of wood for industrial economy and speed of production. Detailed design work began in December 1939. Eleven months later, the prototype Mosquito bomber was towed out of the hanger for its first test flight. But even before the first Mosquito flew, the British government had asked Canada Veneers to furnish such a quantity of aircraft veneer that a tremendous expansion was necessary. By the end of the war, a total of 6,711 Mosquitos had been produced in Britain, Canada and Australia; and production of the fast and versatile aircraft continued well into 1949 and Canada Veneers had become the world's largest supplier of aircraft veneers. The company's expansion was breathtaking: from 180 employees producing 200,000 square feet a week on two floors of the building in 1939, to over 500 employees churning out more than 4,000,000 square feet a week in a jam-packed four-story operation by 1943. The increase in profits, needless to say, was also breathtaking. In the spring of 1943, Cyrus Inches appeared on behalf of the company before the New Brunswick Legislature's Municipalities Committee, during hearings on a bill to fix the tax valuation of the company. Clearly a man whose interest lay in minimizing the profits of the company, Inches nonetheless stated that the aircraft contracts had led to "tremendous" profits. This was a choice of adjectives unique in such circumstances and surely indicative of a level of profit remarkable even in the war years – and astonishing in isolated and unindustrialized New Brunswick.

And not only did the company make those "tremendous" profits, it paid phenomenally low taxes. Because of the tax deal engineered for the company when it was at the brink of bankruptcy, Irving's giant veneer producer enjoyed an assessment of $5,000. School taxes were only slightly less absurd: in 1943 the company, which had been paying $2,000 annually, had its rate raised to $6,500. A bitter blow, no doubt.

If keeping governments from seizing a share of Canada Veneers' wealth posed no problems for Irving, coping with another adversary – one long familiar to him – did. The bitter and continuing labour disputes which were to mark the history of the Canada Veneers plant began in the spring of 1940 when the company was prospering and the workers attempted to unionize. After weeks of negotiations, the company stoutly refused to sign an agreement providing for increased wages and improved working conditions. The stumbling block was a union demand that the company reinstate an employee dismissed, it was claimed, for his union activities. With production at a vital war plant threatened, the federal government stepped in to name a conciliation board under the provisions of the wartime Industrial Disputes Investigation Act. The impending strike was averted and a settlement reached, but each side remained mistrustful of the other. During the three-year agreement minor labour disputes continued to plague the company. When the agreement lapsed and negotiations opened for the second contract in the spring of 1943, the workers were determined to get a better deal from the obviously profitable company than they had on the first contract. Negotiations quickly broke down, and again the dispute went to arbitration. The union demand for a ten cent an hour increase was partially granted by the Regional Wartime Labour Relations Board, but the union was unsatisfied and appealed to the National Board. At the beginning of June negotiations were still dragging on. The frustrated workers, seeking a way to press their demands, struck the plant, but they struck without the permission or support of their union president, George McQueen. McQueen was obviously stung by this blow to his authority. "The strike now in progress at the plant is illegal and wildcat," he said, disclaiming any union participation. But it was an academic distinction, since all the workers in McQueen's local were walking the picket lines. James A. Whitebone, a former city councillor and the president of the Trades and Labour Congress of Canada addressed the workers and urged them to return to work. More sensitive to the plight of Canada Veneers than to that of the workers, he explained to the workers that the Congress had given its pledge to the government that there should be no strikes in essential industries for the duration of the war. "This pledge has never been violated by unions in this district," he added, "and I wish to make it clear that the present regretttable strike is not condoned by the union." Pledges or not, the workers were incensed at the board's offer of a one- to five-cent-an-hour increase on a sliding scale. They decided to hold out for the ten cents an hour they had originally demanded. Meanwhile, company officials sat back to watch. "We'll let the union and strikers thresh it out among themselves," said a spokesman. The next day, H.R. Pettigrove, a federal Department of Labour official, told the striking workers that the board would not have any dealings with them until they returned to work. W.W. Rogers, general manager of the plant, said he "backed up Mr. Pettigrove's stand." At a two and a half hour meeting, the workers voted to return to work, but not before they demanded the resignation of the union president and called new elections.

Their tenacity in the face of opposition from their own union officials and from a wartime government (with its ability to invoke patriotism as a weapon), demonstrates, it would seem, that the Canada Veneers workers were genuinely distressed. It seems clear that they had some indication of the phenomenal profits the company was salting away, profits it was required to share neither with the government nor with its workers.

And the workers remained unhappy, as is evidenced by the continuing disputes at the plant. The union was disturbed about the company's attitude toward its members, and the company increasingly came to regard the union as a disrupting influence. In the spring of 1944, the company attempted to transfer five workers to another department. They refused and were fired. The union walked out for one day in protest. In the spring of 1946, the company dismissed two more employees and a third resigned. This time the workers walked out for three days, claiming that the company was discriminating against the union. Company manager Rogers claimed that there was no union among the employees which was certified by the provincial government and therefore, he said, "there is none which can be recognized by the plant management." The New Brunswick Wartime Labour Relations Board investigated the dispute and ruled that there was no evidence of discrimination against union activities on the company's part, but ordered that the two discharged employees be re-hired with full seniority rights.

That fall the workers walked out again. The union called

the strike after rejecting a Regional Wartime Labour Relations Board recommendation for a six cent an hour wage increase. The union had asked for a ten-cent-an-hour increase, along with various improvements in working conditions. According to a union spokesman, the company was unwilling to make any concessions beyond the recommendations of the board. W.W. Rogers commented that, "if the union was not satisfied, it should have appealed to the National Wartime Labour Relations Board, but instead chose an illegal strike." The strike lasted for a month, but the results were inconclusive: the two sides merely agreed to negotiate.

After further labour difficulty and several layoffs and shutdowns, the longest for a month – necessitated, said Rogers, by a shortage of hardwood veneer logs and gondola cars to transport them – Irving decided to move the company to Pembroke, Ontario, in 1949, where it flourishes today.

But though the company can no longer be found in New Brunswick, its mark remains. For it was largely through the immense amounts of capital generated by the highly profitable business – a business where profits were largely untouched – that Irving was able to finance the astonishing expansion of his empire between the end of the war and the sixties. Another source of that capital, of course, was the makeshift drydock in Boutouche which turned out hundreds of the plywood Minca invasion barges used during that war. And there were undoubtedly others – war is good business. But Canada Veneers was without much doubt a major source of that mammoth capital stockpile which Irving was to utilize so deftly in parlaying his large corporation into a province-dominating empire.

Canada Veneers was an important turning point in the growth of the dinosaur in another way as well. The acquisition of the company led in tactical terms as well as financial ones to the expansion of the Irving holdings in the wood industry. What had begun as a minor addition to the oil and transportation empire became the cornerstone of the developing lumber empire.

As production at the veneer mill reached its peak in late

1942, the problem of ensuring an adequate supply of veneer logs became more acute. Vast tracts of New Brunswick's timberlands had long since been divided up among the province's timber barons and the pulp companies. There were no substantial areas of timberland left. Irving, the relative newcomer, had to import millions of feet of veneer logs from Québec or buy them from the large timber owners in New Brunswick. It was an unenviable position. To an Irving it was a galling one: others controlled the veneer log supply and made the profits from their sale.

In order to become his own supplier, Irving bought the d'Autueil Lumber Company early in 1943. The Québec-based company, with large timber holdings in the eastern part of that province, could provide the veneer logs he needed as well as pulp logs for the mill he had acquired a few months earlier at Dexter, New York. The aquisition of that mill, just across the St. Lawrence River from Kingston, Ontario, had been Irving's first expansion in the forest products industry, but of course was to be far from his last. Nor was it merely an accident; lumber businessmen are still shaking their heads over the skill with which Irving, in a time of wartime restrictions, managed to generate enough American capital to gain control of the Dexter plant.

As the lumber holdings were absorbed, it became increasingly clear that though the d'Autueil Lumber Company was an important addition to the Irving stable of companies, it had certain drawbacks as a supplier for Canada Veneers. The primary one was its distance from the Saint John mill. What Canada Veneers needed was a supply of veneer logs closer to Saint John.

The largest source likely to be available was the vast timberland belonging to the New Brunswick Railway – a company whose history, to the time Irving finally became interested in it, was surely one of the stranger adventures in New Brunswick's long history of government-financed corporate disasters. The company had been incorporated in April 1879 as The New Brunswick and Canada Railway and Land Company

Limited by a handful of the province's foremost businessmen to cash in on the railroad building boom that had seized the country. To help some of its richest businessmen become richer, the provincial government, in its own version of the federal government's gift of 25,000,000 acres of land to the C.P.R., granted the New Brunswick Railway Company a little over 1,600,000 acres of the richest timberland in the province. As was the case in similar deals in other parts of the country, some men made fortunes promoting the company but, despite the government's largesse, twenty years later the New Brunswick Railway Company was bankrupt. It could have been a financial disaster, but then the New Brunswick government has always been quick to recognize its obligation to the province's citizens, particularly when the citizens involved are its wealthiest supporters. With government assistance the New Brunswick Railway Company arranged to lease its 420 miles of track, rolling stock and operating lands for 990 years to the C.P.R. The 1,600,000 acres of rich timberlands, the government decided, would remain in the company's hands and could not be claimed for debt. For the next fifty years, then, the company collected its rent and managed its forests, the only railway company in the country without so much as a handcar. By 1940, the company was worth well over $3,000,000 and for tax purposes decided to reduce its capital and sell off its land. Fraser Companies Limited, owners of twin pulp mills in Edmundston, New Brunswick, and Madawaska, Maine, purchased two blocks of company land: 90,000 acres in the Green River area of Madawaska County, and 623,000 acres in the Tobique territory of Victoria County, both in the northwestern corner of the province near the company's mills. Then in mid-May the *Times-Globe* reported that Irving's d'Autueil Lumber Company had purchased 210,000 acres of New Brunswick Railway Company lands on the Restigouche River in northern New Brunswick. Irving was unavailable for comment, but it was rumoured that he had bought the land for one dollar an acre. Two years later, in the spring of 1945, Irving announced that he had acquired the company itself along with the remaining 700,000 acres of company land. "I have definite plans in mind for the use of the land," he was reported as saying, but he didn't say what they were. Parlaying his gigantic war profits into the deal, Irving had become, in two years, one of the largest timberland owners in the province. It was a prodigious coup: he had control of his own timber supply and by regulating the cutting rate on his own lands could determine the price of timber purchased from smaller suppliers.

Once he had started, Irving rapidly expanded his interests in the timber industry. He bought more timber land in New Brunswick and began buying tracts in the New England states. And then, in the fall of 1946, he bought the Van Buren-Madawaska Corporation lumbermill at Keegan, Maine, the largest sawmill on the east coast. The giant mill had cut more than 80,000,000 board feet of lumber during the war for the United States Army and still employed more than 1,000 men. James A. Gillies, president of the Van Buren-Madawaska Corporation, announced the sale at the beginning of October, but declined to disclose the sale price. Characteristically, Irving made no comment about his huge purchase. Surprisingly, however, the Keegan mill was not to be as important to his timber expansion as its size might have suggested. Much more important was to be a much smaller purchase made earlier that year – the old Port Royal Pulp and Paper Company mill in Fairville, beside the Reversing Falls in the heart of Saint John. For many people in New Brunswick, that one mill has become the central symbol of the Irving empire in the province. They point to pollutants pouring from the mill to cover the mouth of the St. John River with thick milky foam and to the odour from the mill hanging over the city like a pall; an example, they say, of Irving's cavalier disregard for the environment. They point to the almost unbelievably generous subsidies wrung from the municipal and provincial governments as an example of Irving's influence in government and his disregard for the provincial welfare in the pursuit of private profit. But they know, too, that the mill is the largest employer in the city and one of the largest in the province. And as Irving has repeatedly pointed out, he could move it elsewhere. Even his sharpest critics are reluctant to argue that he should do that. So the mill remains in Saint John, a highly visible reminder, at the hub of the Irving empire, of the bittersweet relationship between Irving and the people of his province.

But, perhaps needless to say, the province's attitude toward Irving has not always been ambivalent. When Irving purchased the nearly bankrupt mill in the spring of 1946, the people of Saint John suddenly had hope that he could revive the faltering mill and save its 240 employees from the welfare rolls. And he did save them, though many people think the cost was too high.

The little spit of land known as Union Point, jutting into the mouth of the St. John River, is one of the oldest industrial sites in the city. The first water-powered mill was built there in 1848. Then in 1899, the Cusing interests from the United States, in co-operation with the Partington interests of England, built the pulp mill – one of the first in Canada – which forms the nucleus of the present day mill. In 1916, the property was acquired by the Oxford Pulp and Paper Company of Maine and operated as the Nashwaak Pulp and Paper Company. But with the onset of the Depression in 1929, the mill closed in bankruptcy. Three years later, it was purchased by the Port Royal Pulp and Paper Company of Québec City for $250,000. Even then the city was sufficiently eager to create jobs for the unemployed that in co-operation with the provincial government it garanteed $120,000 worth of the company's bonds. It was an unusual interference with private enterprise, but it set a precedent in concessions to the mill that was to be followed with increasing vigour in succeeding years. The new company prospered and in 1936 new machinery was installed, increasing the capacity of the mill from 85 tons daily to 125 tons. But by the end of the war the company was in financial trouble again. It was forced to shut down for several months at a time because of decreasing markets and a shortage of pulp logs and transportation facilities. When Irving took possession of the mill in mid-March of 1946 he could do little about the inadequate transportation facilities, a problem which was also plaguing Canada Veneers, but the influx of capital did improve the company's financial position. The company, which Irving re-named St. John Sulphite Limited, grew with the ballooning post-war economy until by 1951 Irving was ready for a major $20,000,000 expansion. The company was re-named Irving Pulp and Paper Limited and Irving went to both the city and the provincial legislature that spring for approval of the bill incorporating the new company.

On April 17, a special meeting of the Saint John Municipal Council was held to discuss the municipal concessions that would be written into the bill. The next day it was to come up for second reading in the provincial legislature. It was a contentious bill and the often heated debate lasted for most of the day. Among other things, the Irving company wanted a fixed assessment for thirty years, the authority to dump refuse into the St. John River, virtually unlimited expropriation rights and immunity from any court actions founded on nuisance. Even the Saint John council, which had made some pretty spectacular concessions to companies in the past, found these provisions hard to swallow. Louis Ritchie, representing the company along with Irving himself, told the councillors that from January 1, 1951, the company was willing to pay a fixed annual tax of $35,000 for the next five years, $45,000 for the next ten years, $55,000 for the ten years after that, and then $60,000 annually until 1976, the final five-year period of the agreement. There was some opposition to the taxation schedule the company proposed, but it was surprisingly mild. Three Lancaster councillors said they were in favour of accepting the proposal, but somewhat hesitantly added that since the new mill would increase the burden on Lancaster schools they wished some specific provision could be made so the company would pay school taxes. But, before they could pursue their argument, Councillor A.W. Carton, Warden of the Lancaster Parish, jumped in to take it out of their hands. It was the obligation of the Minister of Education and the province to protect the interests of the schools, he said, ending his councillor's objection. Somewhat circumspectly, Councillor Tippett proposed that the city examine the possibilities of assessments under the Rates and Taxes Act or, warming to his idea, even a percentage of the gross receipts according to the company financial reports. He was answered by Gerald Teed, a private citizen appearing before council, who argued that full taxation on the $20,000,000 investment under the Rates and Taxes Act would be "fantastic". "It would be disturbing," he added, "if taxation matters alone prevented establishment of the industry." But whatever discussion there was of the proposal was soon ended by Ritchie, who reiterated the company's position. "The schedule of rates as proposed," he said, "was the only arrangement that the company could agree on." And that was that: the city would get what taxes the company wanted to pay and no more.

A few of the councillors were worried about some of the other provisions in the bill, but company spokesmen quickly answered their objections. In reply to a question about the effect on fisheries of bark and chemicals being discharged into the river, Mr. Irving said that the chemicals would be diluted by the river waters and were not in themselves harmful to fish. Councillor Prince asked about the purpose of the expropriation clause. "It is the policy of pulp and paper companies to have such rights," replied Mr. Ritchie. Councillor Shanklin said that during a recent trip to the northern sections of the province he had noticed a severe odour in the area of similar mills and wondered if the same could be expected in Saint John. Frank J. Lang, managing director of the company, said the mill would smell; there was no practical way to remove it. In areas where mills caused great growth and prosperity, he said, no one complained about the odour.

But by this point in the meeting none of the councillors were prepared to object strenuously to anything. Earlier, Mr. Irving had explained his company's position in terms that even the simplest councillor could understand. He began with the subtlety he reserved for such occasions by reminding the councillors that he had considered several sites for the mill including St. Stephen and Grand Falls before deciding to try to locate in Saint John. His firm had the interests of Saint John foremost, he said. "A lot of trouble in New Brunswick and Saint John was due to a lack of industry," read the report of his comments in that evening's *Times-Globe.* "A start on getting new industry had to be made some place and he suggested that it be made with the proposed pulp and paper mill. What the company was seeking, was what it felt was required." The outcome of the meeting was never in doubt. The council approved the bill in principle unanimously, including the fixed taxation proposal.

The following day, April 18, the bill was introduced into the legislature for second reading. Opposition Leader Hugh Mackay suggested that the bill might be modified by the legislature to exclude some provisions that particularly bothered him, specifically the right to discharge wastes into the St. John River, and the broad expropriation powers. "I don't want to obstruct the Irving interests from building their new pulp mill at the mouth of the river," he said, "but I feel that some things contained in the bill could be modified so as to ease its way through." Premier McNair said he understood the bill had awakened some public interest and anxiety, but he assured the legislature that the Irving bill was much like bills already passed incorporating other pulp and paper companies. Referring to the section permitting the company to dump its wastes into the river, the premier said he thought the provincial legislature might not have the authority or right to deal with the matter. "Maybe this comes under federal jurisdiction," he said, although he wasn't sure that it did. Besides, he went on to say, he didn't know who would undertake to approach the Irving company for the purpose of carrying out Mr. Mackay's suggestion. He would not care to do it, and he was sure the Opposition Leader would not want to. The premier concluded by saying he thought the best plan would be to let the matter takes its course. Lest he be misunderstood, the Opposition Leader jumped up to clarify his position."I'm not protesting this measure," he said, explaining "I thought we might save an uproar over it later on; the less the better."

There was an uproar, mild and shortlived, but an uproar nevertheless. The next day the bill – the most contentious of the sitting, said the *Times-Globe* – came up before the Corporations Committee. If the bill was to be changed, it would have to be changed here. When the committee convened at 3.30 that afternoon every seat in the room was filled and the doorways were crowded with spectators. It promised to be an interesting afternoon. Louis Richie, who, accompanied by Cyrus Inches and K.C. Irving, represented the company, was the first to testify. He explained to the committee the effects of the most contentious sections in the bill. The pollution from the mill would be minimal, he said; only about one one-thousandth of the 25,000,000 gallons of water the mill would use each day would go into the river "resulting in almost no contamination." Besides, he added, the great turbulence at the Reversing Falls would cause fusion to be universal. "The discharge into the river would not be poisonous and the proportion would be so small that it would not have any effect on fish. . . . The mill is now discharging waste into the St. John River," he concluded, "but it would be well to have the authority." Premier McNair noted that this was one of the clauses that had caused considerable public concern. He said he understood the main objection was in connection with fish life which was clearly a federal matter. In any case, he added, the inclusion of that provision was of really no effect, and he was inclined to think that the section should be deleted. Ritchie conferred with Irving and came back to inform the committee that the president of the company had agreed to the deletion of the clause. As Mr. Ritchie had pointed out earlier, it would be well to have the authority, but the company intended to continue dumping its wastes into the river in any case.

As far as the smell from the mill was concerned, Mr. Ritchie assured the committee that the "company would use the most modern methods and keep odours down to a minimum." Ralph J. Broderick, representing the Saint John Real Estate Owner's Association, thought it should be a definite statutory duty for the company to take all steps possible to eliminate noxious odours and vapours. There was some discussion of the smell from the mill, but the feeling of the committee members seemed to be expressed by the Liberal member from Saint John County, H.C. Atkinson, who reminded the committee that this was "the biggest industrial plum that has fallen our way for some time." He added that he had worked in the odour of pulp mills for thirty-one years and it hadn't affected him. "All pulp mills have odours," he said, "and the people will just have to get used to them."

Perhaps more important was the expropriation clause, about which, Premier McNair said, "considerable interest had developed and objections had been taken." "The answer," he said, "was that the objectives for which the powers could be exercised were restricted and that the approval of the Lieutenant-Governor in Council was required." He said he thought the provision followed very closely other similar legislation. Few others at the hearing could share his naive complacency. Councillor E.A. Whitebone of the Saint John Municipal Council argued that the right of property was a fundamental one and while there were precedents of companies in New Brunswick being granted expropriation powers, this did not make such measures any better. "If industry is to be obtained at the expense of losing human rights, then it is better not to have it," he concluded. Ralph J. Broderick, as a representative of the Saint John Real Estate Owner's Association was, perhaps understandably, the most outspoken critic of the expropriation section. "By expropriating large timber limits," he argued, "the company would be in a position to dictate prices on the pulp market. It could force the small producer to accept a certain price by threatening to cut its own timber." "I am in favour of the company acquiring specific lands," he said, "but it should not be given a blanket authority."

But the clause in the expropriation section that clearly caused the greatest consternation was sub-section 7 which provided that the sheriff "shall take with him sufficient assistance for the purpose and shall put down such resistance and opposition and shall put the company, or such person acting

113

for it, in possession thereof. . . . " Mr. Broderick argued that under this section he thought the company could have "special police sworn in as sheriffs to put down opposition. It envisions the possibility of riots and bloodshed, with the sheriff organizing posses to enforce the provision." "Granting such powers," he said, "should not even be considered." But, of course, it was being considered, as was the provision that authorized the company to give the owner a mere ten days notice that his property had been expropriated before it took possession. Moreover, the act included no provision requiring the company to first make an offer of purchase. At this point, Premier McNair agreed that the powers under the bill "were rather broad" and perhaps should be "limited to specific purposes."

The debate raged on in the crowded committee room for five and a half hours, while normal house business, including the budget debate, was completely forgotten. When the hearings ended late that evening, after the bill was ordered to private session, several amendments had been made. The section that would have permitted the company to expropriate lands "generally for and in connection with all the powers and purposes of the company" was deleted, as was the clause permitting the sheriff to take with him "sufficient assistance" to put down any opposition from the owner of expropriated land. Some of the most objectionable aspects of the bill had been removed or amended, but letters and telegrams protesting various sections of the bill poured into the legislators in undiminished volume. Despite the unprecedented public criticism, however, five days later, when the bill came up for third and final reading, it was passed without a dissenting vote.

During the private session held by the Corporations Committee, some amendments were agreed on, but the substance of the bill remained the same. The company could now expropriate whatever land it "shall deem necessary or useful." What the company could consider necessary or useful was specified in six sub-sections. Unfortunately, the limiting sub-sections did little to limit the broad expropriation powers since the company could deem it useful to expropriate land in connection with "mills and ancillary works," "driving, sorting, booming, storing and piling logs and pulpwood," "pipe lines," "flumes," "railway lines," "and roads." The company could still "divert the flow of any watercourse . . . to such an extent as it shall deem necessary or useful." It could still enter on any lands to make surveys and collect data, but now it could only do so for the purposes of expropriation or water diversion and would be liable for any damages caused when it did enter. While the committee agreed to the fixed tax rate the company had proposed, it added a section requiring a payment of $200,000 over a twenty-year period in school taxes. But the section exempting the company from any action founded on nuisance was retained.

And so the bill was passed incorporating the industry which was to become for most New Brunswickers the central symbol of Irving's domination of the province. During the next two decades the mill would be expanded again and again, demanding more and more concessions from the city and the province. Over and over, the precedents set in 1951, and the capital produced originally by Canada Veneers and the business boom caused by the war, parlayed into expansions of the mill, into water-rates and tax concessions. That process finally produced the mill which now stands at the nerve centre of the dinosaur, dominating the mouth of New Brunswick's main waterway. But the financial and legal groundwork for that growth were all there by 1951.

And as early as the fifties it was clear that Irving was the figure to be reckoned with in the New Brunswick timber industry. With an almost total control of the timber resources of the lower three hundred miles of the St. John River, with timber holdings so vast he could literally set his own price for pulpwood, with the liquid capital to buy whatever was needed to complete the vertical integration of his corporate structure, and with the political skills and influence to wring necessary concessions from government or to freeze out new competition, Irving's domination of his province was nearly total. The dinosaur bestriding the New Brunswick landscape in the early fifties must have looked virtually invulnerable to outside companies thinking of locating in that province. And though there were chinks in its armoured skin, they were hardly obvious then; it seemed to New Brunswickers that, for good or ill, they would have to get used to living in its shadow.

CHAPTER FOUR

Base Metals and Base Politics

The history of New Brunswick in the 1960s is inextricably bound up with base metals and wood. It is perhaps typical of that province – always second best, always slightly inferior in self-esteem if not in fact – that its crucial decade should revolve around spruce and balsam, lead and zinc, and not around mahogany or gold.

But if the materials at stake were unromantic, the people weren't: and if it is ever to be clear how French and English, government and business, rich and poor manage through conflict and misunderstanding to keep New Brunswick impoverished and second-rate, the tragedy of the 1960s must be understood. The central character, as always, is the Irving corporate entity. In the years between 1960 and 1971, however, another character almost muscled Irving off the stage: the gutsy little Acadian premier of the province, Louis Robichaud, who during the last few years of the decade fought the Irving dinosaur to a bloody draw. And of all the bones over which they fought, the largest and most contentious one was the mineral-rich rock of the North Shore.

When William Hussey first discovered that there were base metals – mainly, it seemed, iron – in the hills of the Bathurst area on New Brunswick's poverty-stricken North Shore,

Kenneth Colin Irving, then three years old, was living in Bouc-touche, another village on that same North Shore. At their maturity, both of those North Shore phenomena were to affect the life of New Brunswick in ways that could hardly have been foretold in 1902. About the only thing that could have been foretold accurately even then was that if economic power was going to be generated among these fishing villages and lumber camps, it would not be wielded by the Acadian majority of the population.

While little Kenneth Colin began to show promise fairly early in his life, Bathurst Iron Mines was hardly what might be called a precocious child; for fifty years, while editorial colum-nists, Chamber of Commerce types, and encyclopedia writers enthused lukewarmly about the mineral resources of northern New Brunswick, Bathurst remained something less than a decisive factor in New Brunswick's economic life. This was the state of affairs when, in 1952, an itinerant mining promoter named Matthew James Boylen went to New York with a map purporting to show the precise location of a large base metals deposit in northern New Brunswick. Somehow, against what looks even by hindsight to be hopeless odds, Boylen raised a million dollars and took it to the North Shore to sink it into the ground. Following his map, he sunk eleven holes and found nothing.

No matter how many second-rate movies you've seen, it doesn't seem likely that Boylen would go on and sink one last hole and strike paydirt, but that's what happened. And it was spectacular paydirt: samples indicated values of 28,000 tons of a complex lead-zinc-silver ore a vertical foot. Still following that second-rate movie scenario, Boylen swore his crews to secrecy, staked nine hundred claims in the names of various companies – all his – and let the news out. Stocks in northern New Brunswick mining companies – most of them Boylen's – ran wild. His New Larder "U" company, for instance, whose claim was some distance from the main body, traded 1,200,000 shares in a day, and in less than a month went from twelve cents a share to $2.65. When Boylen set up Brunswick Mining and Smelting, to acquire the old Bathurst Iron Mines, and assembled all his claims under its aegis, he offered the shares at $10.00 par value to start; they were promptly bid to $21.75. Boylen was a made man. Penny mining stocks came into vogue again. And the dormant North Shore economy stirred, grunted and mumbled in its sleep.

But by 1960 it hadn't even rolled over, much less awakened; and in spite of effusions in the press about the mammoth mineral wealth of the area, poor Acadians still fished, or cut pulp for the mills, or lived on the dole in appalling shacks in the back country, growing up malnourished and undereducated, isolated and exploited – because, as even the people who had bid Boylen's stock up knew, newly-discovered ore bodies usually pay off only for the speculators. It's easy to buy and sell stocks on the basis of what the metallurgists say is in the ground; it's a far different business to get it out, refine it and sell it. It takes not only capital, but commitment and guts and hard work, especially when the body poses as many problems as the complex Brunswick lode did. Every such discovery faces a series of related dangers: first, that the speculators will pull their capital out before any mining can be done at all; second, that the market for metals won't support the mining (this is especially likely when a complex ore makes refinement a sophisticated and expensive problem, as with Brunswick); and third, that the mine will remain merely a shipping point from which ore is sent to concentrators and smelters elsewhere, producing no permanent economic effect on the area around it. A classic case of this, of course, is the "uranium cities" of northern Ontario, where the ore was exhausted and the whole area abandoned by the companies within a few years.

Brunswick had overcome the first hurdle, partly because M.J. Boylen was something more than merely a promoter and had remained interested in the company, and partly because the company ultimately came under the control of a large, stable corporation, St. Joseph's Lead of New York. But it would be hard to find a better example of the unfortunate effects of foreign ownership on an economy than St. Joseph's control of Brunswick Mining and Smelting. St. Joseph's didn't want concentrates from New Brunswick further deflating the already limp American base metals market; on the other hand it didn't want to give up the concentrates to European smelting operations (someday they might need the Brunswick lode); and of course they didn't want to give up control as long as keeping it cost the company a minimum. So St. Joseph's Lead sat on the deposit – as Liberal member of the opposition in the provincial legislature M.J. Gallant said in April 1959, "a dog in a manger". As a representative of the North Shore, and as a member of a party that traditionally found its base of power among the dispossessed Acadians of that area, Gallant had some reason for pique. In April 1958, St. Joseph's had simply closed down the operation, forcing 175 men out of work, because, they said, the base metals market was deflated and because there were difficulties in financing a smelter – a smelter that St. Joseph's wasn't particularly interested in in any case. The mine lay dormant for almost two years, until the winter of 1959, when rumours began flying that Brunswick would start up again, on the basis of a revival of the base metals market and new management; the rumours had it that St. Joseph's was no longer in complete control, that Sogemines Limited, the Canadian offshoot of the international Belgian giant, the Société Générale des Minerais, had obtained nominal control and were interested in shipping concentrates to their own European smelters.

But Sogemines and St. Joseph's did not reckon on the arrival on the New Brunswick scene of another North Shore phenomenon, one that was to prove much stronger than they could imagine, and that would drive St. Joseph's out of Brunswick Mining and Smelting altogether within a couple of years. In June 1960, Louis J. Robichaud, to the surprise of almost everybody in the province, was elected premier of New Brunswick. For the next ten years, he and K.C. Irving were to be the pivotal figures in the fortunes of that mammoth deposit of lead-zinc-silver ore, as of everything else in New Brunswick.

Even the multinational corporations were to take a back seat to the gigantic struggle that was to take place in New Brunswick during the sixties, a struggle that would involve the whole economic and political life of the province, but that would begin and end in the fortunes of Brunswick Mining and Smelting.

Though the struggle climaxed in the sixties it had its roots long before the election of Louis Robichaud; in fact, his election, like that of previous New Brunswick premiers, seemed to usher in a period of honeymoon between the Irving empire and the government. From the election of Allison Dysart in 1935 – also from Bouctouche and a pallbearer at the funeral of Irving's father – to 1960 the pattern had remained similar. At the beginning, the new government would see clearly that co-operating with Irving was the only way to bring industrial progress to New Brunswick, and would only gradually discover issues on which Irving's definition of progress and the government's would differ. Conflict would ensue; Irving's support (Irving supports all governments, Tory or Liberal; though he himself is a staunch Liberal, he attended Diefenbaker rallies in 1957 and 1958) would wither; and the government would be defeated, often publicly ascribing the loss to Irving's opposition. Arthur – the most political of Irving's three sons – once said in a moment of incaution that his father had never lost an election in New Brunswick, and until 1967 that remained true.

It is often said that everyone in New Brunswick – with the possible exceptions of Louis Robichaud and K.C. Irving – was surprised by Robichaud's 1960 victory. Campaigning on almost no platform other than his fiery oratory, the brash young lawyer from Richibucto – a few miles from Irving's Bouctouche – seemed merely another in the series of Acadian sacrificial victims the Liberals had served up to the St. John River power base. New Brunswick had never elected an Acadian premier, though it was a Liberal tradition to alternate the leadership between Acadians and English-speaking New Brunswickers. Running against eight years of slow but apparently solid economic growth (much of it caused by K.C. Irving's entrepreneurial skill, and backed by the government), Robichaud had as issues only his proposal to modernize New Brunswick's archaic liquor laws (a contentious issue at best, and one that has traditionally tended to split New Brunswick on French-English lines) and a proposal to have the province take over the payment of health insurance premiums.

But behind the scenes, the issues were slightly different. Hugh John Flemming, the incumbent Tory premier, had promised Irving a ninety-acre slice of land on Courtenay Bay in Saint John for expansion of his recently-acquired Saint John Shipbuilding and Dry Dock. But Flemming was attempting to find some way out of the commitment so that the government could give the land to the newly-conceived Rothesay Paper Company, a scheme of a consortium of companies – primarily Sogemines – to construct a paper mill in competition with Irving's at the mouth of the St. John River. This displeased Irving on two counts – first, because he felt he had been given an unequivocal commitment to that land (the government later denied the commitment, and it will probably never be known just how unequivocal it really was); second, because whatever his protestations to the contrary Irving did not want competition for the water, pulp wood and labour force of Saint John and southern New Brunswick. As long as his was the only mill at the mouth of the river, the river was effectively his from the Fraser mill at Edmundston on down, three hundred miles to the Bay of Fundy. Because of the nature of its incorporation and site, the Irving Pulp and Paper Company had expropriation rights anywhere along the river, could not be sued for any damage caused by its log drives and – most important – could pretty well set its own price for pulp in the whole of southern New Brunswick. If the independent pulp cutters demanded more, Irving could always cut his own pulp off the vast tracts of New Brunswick Railway land that he had bought after the Second World War. Thus, throughout the spring of 1959, the Irving interests fought to block passage of the bill incorporating Rothesay Paper in New Brunswick and, failing that, to

122

keep Rothesay from having the protections Irving Pulp and Paper had been enjoying since 1951, especially the right to expropriate and the protection from being sued for creating nuisance (for instance, making someone's home uninhabitable with pulp mill gas). And failing *that,* one could keep Rothesay out by not allowing them that choice land on Courtenay Bay.

The media supported Irving vociferously. At the time, the Saint John radio station and four of the five English daily papers in the province were his, and the fifth, the Fredericton *Daily Gleaner,* was owned by the Irving-worshipping Brigadier Michael Wardell, who later sold the paper to Irving. A special page one editorial in the *Gleaner* was read into the debate in the legislature by young Robichaud, then Opposition Leader. "New Brunswick owes him [Irving] much," said the *Gleaner* – and Robichaud. "New Brunswick must be loyal to its old association. It should not endanger a great industry to placate a newcomer." Robichaud went on, "I think that the view of one man in this province, Mr. K.C. Irving, should be heard in this legislature, as he has done so much for this province." If it had not been clear before that Irving's golden ball was now being carried by the opposition, the debate of April 6 in the Legislative Assembly made it manifest: it was Robichaud who read into the record Irving's 250-word telegram attacking the legislation.

It was even clearer during the provincial election of 1960, when Irving pulled his support away from the Flemming government and threw it to the young Robichaud, who unashamedly worshipped Irving, who shared his Kent County background, who had grown up surrounded by the Irving success story. Whether Irving's influence on that election was actually decisive will probably never be known, but Arthur Irving, at any rate, counted it as a victory for his father. In any case, Irving's newspapers were indeed surprisingly cordial toward the young Liberal leader, whose campaign was unusually well-organized and well-financed. And one of the first acts of the new government was to announce that it intended to keep the previous government's commitment to give the ninety-acre site on Courtenay Bay to Irving's Saint John Shipbuilding and Dry Dock, and not to Rothesay Paper. It was also about this time that Robichaud, having discovered that the Dry Dock needed business, called Lester Pearson personally and got Irving two contracts from the government.

Flushed with the success of establishing a good working relationship with Irving, Robichaud's government turned to another vexing problem: St. Joseph's Lead's decision not to develop the Brunswick Mining and Smelting ore body. In the Liberal's "election manifesto" of the previous May, the party had gone on record as favouring a drastic change in the way mineral resources in New Brunswick were handled. "New Brunswick has one of the largest bodies of base metal deposits in the world," the document pointed out. It went on with a curtness unusual in such documents, "Their exploitation to date has benefitted only the stock promoters. We will take appropriate legal action to provide for the development of our mineral resources in the interest of New Brunswickers. Our minerals will not be allowed to lie dormant while other provinces push ahead." Robichaud knew that the only way to have any long-term effect on the economy of the North Shore was to establish some kind of permanent industry around the mine – and that even mining the ore and shipping it to smelters was hardly a permanent industry, or one with much of a multiplier effect. A smelter and associated chemical or steel industry would be, he thought, ideal; but the first step in accomplishing this would have to be – as it is rumoured a cabinet member said at the time – to get the lead out. St. Joseph's Lead had somehow to be forced out of Brunswick, and someone who would develop the potential of the mine enticed in. But who? Development on the scale envisioned by Louis Robichaud would obviously require a mammoth capital investment, a willingness to take a daring gamble, and a commitment to expanding in New Brunswick rather than elsewhere.

Given Irving's position in the province, not to mention his relationship with the government, of course, there was never any real doubt. But the mechanics were complex; and in 1960 it was not at all clear that Irving was even interested in getting into mining. In 1938 he and Frank Brennan had become involved with Sogemines in gold exploration, especially in Nova Scotia, but nothing had come of that venture. So it was not as obvious then as it is by hindsight that it was going to have to be Irving.

When the government decided to tell Boylen to get rid of St. Joseph's and get some new partners who would develop the mine and build a smelter, they were taking a chance. They were warned at the time (by no less a personage than Lord Beaverbrook) not to let Irving, who already controlled most of New Brunswick's economy, to get hold of this field as well; they were also warned that Boylen would take some watching. What seems to have been envisioned was that Boylen would emerge in control, but with Irving as a watchdog. It turned out, as a longtime Robichaud associate later said, that it wasn't Boylen that needed watching. But at first it seemed that Boylen would remain the dominant figure in the history of the Brunswick enterprise. Still deeply involved in the company, and quick enough to capitalize on the government's actions, Boylen organized East Coast Smelting and Chemical Company to explore the possibility of a smelter. Sensing, with his promoter's instinct, that the government simply could not allow such a venture to fail, he offered St. Joseph's Lead $10, 500,00 for their interest, and got a promise from the government that they would guarantee capitalization of a smelter if he could raise the money in forty-five days.

Part of the smelter problem was not financial at all: because the Brunswick ore was so complex, smelting it would be difficult – perhaps even impossible – and new smelting techniques would have to be worked out in the remote wilderness of northern New Brunswick. Some of the most vivid memories of the people involved in the Robichaud government at this time are of the incredible rapidity with which Irving himself and his organization familiarized themselves with the complexities of base metals smelting as they, Boylen's group, and others, assessed the risks. Finally it was decided that the new Imperial

Smelting process would solve the problems, and in June of 1961 a consortium composed of Irving, Boylen's Maritimes Mining, and three companies associated with the giant Bolivian mining company, Patiño, bought out St. Joseph's interest in Brunswick for Boylen's offer of $10,500,000. Under the terms of the purchase, Irving put up $2,520,000 to buy a twenty-four per cent interest in St. Joseph's share, while Maritimes Mining had a forty-six per cent share for $4,820,000 and Patiño's three companies – Patiño Enterprises Inc., Patiño Canada Limited, and Nipissing Mines, all had a ten per cent share. The new president of the company was E.R.E. Carter, a Patiño executive.

Now that control was theirs, the new management still needed $20,000,000 in capitalization to get into production. Irving suggested that Sogemines, who still had an interest in the company, might be approached for some and that he himself might be willing to put up some. Ultimately a deal was worked out which involved Sogemines buying $11,500,000 worth in American funds of first mortgage bonds and Irving, through his Engineering Consultants Limited of Saint John, $8,000,000 worth in Canadian funds. Arrangements were then made for the government to guarantee financing of the smelter construction, and by November Robichaud could triumphantly announce that the North Shore was going to be awakened – by his government.

The Throne Speech which opened the legislature that November 15 said that since the government was "firm in its determination that the rich mineral resources of the province will be developed and processed to provide impetus to our economy and a good livelihood for thousands more of our people," that arrangements had been made for "the orderly development of an integrated mine, mill, smelter and chemical complex to utilize the vast base metals deposits of the Bathurst-Newcastle area," a program which would "place New Brunswick in the forefront of mineral development in Canada." The legislative session which followed was to be a busy one.

Three things had to be done that fall to get Brunswick going. Brunswick itself had to be reincorporated by an act of the legislature; so did East Coast Smelting and Chemical Company; and the financing of the whole deal had to be approved. And it had to be done quickly. Within two days of the Throne Speech, then, and riding on the crest of the enthusiasm in the press about Brunswick's (read Irving's) plans for the North Shore, Bills Nos. 4 ("An Act Relating to East Coast Smelting and Chemical Company Limited") and 5 ("An Act Relating to Brunswick Mining and Smelting Corporation Limited") were given first reading in the legislature. Everything seemed to be going smoothly; it was not until the bills reached the Corporations Committee, after second reading, that the sparks began to fly. When they did, they were so thick that, after two days of wrangling, Irving himself appeared before the committee.

By this time there was a bit of morning-after coolness in the relations between Irving and the government. The government had, while honouring its land commitment to the Dry Dock, managed to unearth another tract of land, disentangle it from a complex legal situation, sweeten the offer with guarantees of water and of steam from a nearby generating plant, and in a long, painful, cliff-hanging process, sell Rothesay on the idea of locating at the mouth of the St. John, thereby guaranteeing competition for logs, land, and labour. "We welcome competition," Irving had said again and again, but he had fought for years to keep Rothesay out of New Brunswick. So while he could hardly have been entirely pleased with the government, he couldn't admit it publicly. Even so, of course, the government knew where he stood, and had managed to go ahead with the Rothesay deal against his presumed wishes only because certain members of the government were painfully aware that if this deal fell through – as the Lepreau paper mill had fallen through five years before – all outside capital would give up on New Brunswick, deciding that the province was indeed Irving's fief.

But during the Corporations Committee hearings and the debate in the legislature over passage of the two bills Irving and the government were models of unanimity. And, ironically, the main issues of contention included precisely the ones Irving and Robichaud had just fought out in connection with the Rothesay Paper incorporation: the clause protecting the company from being sued for nuisance, and the right of expropriation. But this time the two Kent County boys were on the other side.

The two bills were models of the kind of giveaway that industry has traditionally been able to promote from the governments of New Brunswick. They included, along with the now traditional nuisance and expropriation clauses, clauses allowing the companies to enter into long-term tax and water agreements with local authorities, and a clause giving East Coast Smelting, for ten years, the exclusive right to smelt lead and zinc concentrates in the province (as long as it did so "competitively" and did not refuse the concentrates of other mines), and a two-year exclusive right "to commence and proceed with the construction and direction within the Province of New Brunswick of a smelter designed to smelt and process lead and zinc concentrates", provided it start building no later than 31 December 1963. Since one couldn't ship concentrates out of the province, East Coast was given a pretty considerable competitive edge. But the government, in the traditional manner of governments of New Brunswick, saw the chance to create this large industry as worth the concessions; and after three stormy days in the Corporations Committee and a surprisingly contentious third reading in the legislature, the bills were passed unanimously. Almost all of those who appeared to oppose the bill – and there were so many that the Corporations Committee had to move out of its usual committee room into the legislative chamber – reminded the legislature that they were not opposed to the principle of the bill, or to the industry, or to the idea of special privileges, or even to the unusual procedure of granting, in an act of the legislature, the $20,000,000 bond guarantee. Each of them opposed merely some specific section of the law that might affect him; the broadest objections were lodged by conservation groups such as the Miramichi Salmon Association. Others, like Heath Steele, a mine on the Miramichi, complained merely that they might be held captive to a competitive company under the terms of the exclusivity clause. But the most characteristic attitude was that expressed by E.G. Byrne, a Bathurst lawyer who was to be a member of the supporting cast in almost every conflict during the decade. In this case he was representing the Canadian Metal Mining Association. He asked that some provision be made for some payment of damages, but argued vociferously in favour of the nuisance protection in general. When a conservation representative proposed an amendment regarding injunctions in case of stream pollution, Byrne said he was sympathetic, but that an industry using millions of gallons of water daily shouldn't be subject to the risk of being closed indefinitely, arguing that a choice would have to be made between helping industry and protecting "small groups interested in fishing." "I'm not in favour of pollution," he said, "but we can't stand in the way of development. We'll have some pollution, since the water has to go somewhere."

Finally, the exclusivity clause was softened somewhat and the nuisance clause amended slightly to read, "No action founded on nuisance shall lie against the Company or any Subsidiary *except with the consent of the Attorney General.*" But no substantive changes were made, and the mood during the later sessions of the committee was a mellow one, with K.C. Irving reiterating his praise of the Robichaud government for promoting this mammoth industry. But perhaps Irving's most characteristic utterance involved the nuisance clause. He insisted that the company was prepared to pay for actual damage created, but the nuisance clause was necessary to avoid petty interference with operations. "Some people might not like the industry," he said, "and keep active in the courts. We want to avoid this. If we are not good citizens the legislature can repeal or change the law, if we become real nuisances, but we don't want to be annoyed for no good reason." He also pointed out – with, perhaps, some vindictiveness – that the same clause had been included in the Rothesay deal.

He conceded that the smelter smoke "on some days" might make it "a little unpleasant", but reiterated the company's willingness to pay for "actual damage". Byrne argued against the necessity of the clause, pointing out that Bathurst Power and Paper had not had a nuisance suit in fifty years even though the mill at times "gave off such an odour that it was almost impossible to breathe." Characteristically, there was no answer to this and the citizens of Bathurst were left to breathe as well as they might.

The only issue that generated any public furor at all in the entire controversy was one particularly characteristic of the deliberations of bodies like the New Brunswick legislature, one generated entirely by the desire of each side of the house to score points in debate on the other. During the Friday hearings in the Corporations Committee, it became apparent that the government was not certain whether the security for their guarantee was the $51,000,000 total investment at Brunswick, or merely the smelter, which was at that time projected to be worth $28,000,000. The opposition pounced on this mistake, and it became the major issue in the Legislative Assembly debate over the third reading of the bill. C.B. Sherwood, then leader of the opposition, charged that Robichaud at first said that the security would be $51,000,000 and then that it would be the $28,000,000 smelter. The vitriolic stupidity of the ensuing debate is unexceeded – though certainly not unrivalled – in the annals of the New Brunswick legislature, with much embarrassingly crude controversy over Robichaud's diminutive size, including Tory G. Everett Chalmers of Fredericton referring to Robichaud as a "chimpanzee". But Robichaud had the last word; at the height of the shouting match, he scored match point: "Vote against it if you dare. I double dare you to vote against it".

Dumb, but effective. No one was going to vote against it. And the furor about the "mistake" effectively muffled any genuine controversy there might have been. The sort of debate indulged in makes it difficult to infer that any of the legislators were bright enough to have planned such a tactic, but it worked as well as if it had been planned. The bills passed and the guarantee was made. And the deal worked out to everybody's advantage – or so it seemed. Irving's firm, Engineering Consultants Limited, got to build the mine and mill through tune-up, and received an eight per cent of cost fee for management services. Sogemines got all the concentrates from the mine and mill until the smelter was ready, and any surplus after that. And the government got all the political advantages that came with the development – the propaganda value of any industrial development, especially on the desperate North Shore; the confidence and co-operation of K.C. Irving; and all the little patronage and perquisites that come with any major construction work. For a while, everyone was happy.

But no one, of course, was satisfied. Irving could not have been happy in less than full control of Brunswick – especially because his major partners included foreign corporations, both involved in Rothesay Paper. Irving was never happy unless he had full control, and unless he was expanding on all fronts. "You've got to keep going," he said once. "Expansion is the thing. The trouble with many businessmen is that when they have made some progress they sit back and take a rest. We can't progress while standing still."

Ideally, what Irving almost certainly wanted was complete ownership of Brunswick. That, of course, was impossible; there simply wasn't the capital available to him. But almost immediately, it appears, he began buying stock, through subsidiaries, in companies with interests in Brunswick, assembling an ever larger proportion of Brunswick's shares. And on October 31, 1964, just about three years after Irving's first venture into the mining field, the *Financial Post* broke the story that Irving had emerged in control of Brunswick. A Toronto Stock Exchange filing statement, they had discovered, showed Irving as the holder of almost 1,700,000 shares of Key Anacon mines; and moreover Kent Lines (an Irving Company) was buying $900,000 worth of Key Anacon debentures, which would be convertible into 900,000 shares. Converted, they would give Irving a forty-seven per cent interest in Key Anacon. Added to their estimate of Irving's other interests in Brunswick, he would then have about thirty-eight per cent, with M.J. Boylen holding a twenty-nine per cent interest.

Much of this argument was hypothetical, of course; Irving by this time in his career was adept at hiding his tracks in the inter-corporate thicket. But it was hard to hide a dinosaur in a thicket even the size of Brunswick – and whether Irving was in actual numerical control or not (he was later to deny that he ever had "control"), the corporation certainly began acting like an Irving corporation in about 1964, with plans for mammoth expansion announced right and left. There was to be an $18,000,000 chemical and fertilizer complex (Belledune Fertilizer), which would use, among other things, sulphuric acid from the smelter; there was to be a $64,000,000 steel plant (Bay Steel) to fabricate the metal right on the spot, or possibly in Saint John; there was to be a $20,000,000 investment in ships and docks; there was to be another open-pit mine for New Brunswick. "We can't progress standing still."

At the same time, Irving was also quietly gaining control of First Maritime Mining, the company which, under the name Maritimes Mining, had been Boylen's principal instrument in the Brunswick transactions. On the surface, things were going well for Irving and Brunswick. But behind the scenes there were problems. The smelter was in trouble, both technically and financially. In early 1963, well before the deadline for starting on the smelter, Irving, Brunswick President E.R.E. Carter, and John D. Park, Irving's new right-hand man and the president of Engineering Consultants Ltd., had gone to see Robichaud to ask for an extension on the deadline for the smelter. There were technical problems, they said, that should be solved in the planning stage rather than while the thing was being built. Moreover, it was already clear that it was going to cost more than $20,000,000 and it would be folly to go ahead without making sure of financing.

But the government wasn't having any. Politically, and economically, they needed that smelter. They needed it at least partly because, at the time, they were fighting an election on the issue of their concessions to the proposed South Nelson Forest Products mill, and the opposition's main charge was that there had been no genuine guarantee that Cartiere del Timavo, the Italian backers of South Nelson, were actually going to build a mill; that they were likely simply to cut the pulp and ship it out of the country, creating no permanent industry. To lose the smelter start at the same time, to back down on a precisely analogous situation, would have been political suicide. The government had to insist that the deadline be met, come hell or high water.

In September, after the government had been returned, Irving went back, but to no avail. The government was committed. Not only was it committed to a smelter, but to a smelter on the North Shore; a report from the New York firm of metallurgical engineers, Singmaster and Brayer, recommending that the smelter be built in Saint John, cut no ice with the government. It was the economy of the North Shore that needed reviving, they said, not that of Saint John. And so, as Irving increased his capital investment in Brunswick and tightened his grip on control, he increasingly found himself in conflict with a government which had invested a large proportion of its political capital in the success of the smelter. And political capital is one stock Irving doesn't understand at all.

Moreover, there was an increasing antipathy between Robichaud and Irving, based partly on continuing conflict over Brunswick, over Rothesay Paper, and probably over South Nelson Forest Products, a development that Irving cannot have been happy with. It's clear that the developing dislike went further than that, though, to become almost a symbol of the kinds of division that have bedevilled New Brunswick throughout its history. On the one hand, a tall, spare, ascetic Presbyterian; shrewd, cool, morally rigorous, hardworking, who doesn't smoke or drink or swear. An archetypal English Protestant. And on the other? Short, slick, sweaty, hard-drinking, feisty Louis Robichaud – a showman, an orator, a salesman, a gladhander: a politician. And typically North Shore

French. You can't argue that there was ever prejudice on either side; both grew up in Kent County; both had friends from the opposite group. But they were opposites, and no amount of mutual admiration in 1960 could bridge the long gap that opened up when Louis saw a political advantage and Kenneth a financial one.

But in 1963 not many outside the inner circle saw the gap widening and K.C. Irving was still identified in the media as the power behind the Liberal government in New Brunswick. When he denied it, saying that nothing could be further from the truth, pundits chuckled, not believing that he was stating the plain truth. Even as late as June 1965, when Robichaud announced an ultimatum to mining companies in the province to "develop or get out", it was widely reported that the government was talking to companies who were slow to follow Brunswick's lead. It was not at all clear that the ultimatum applied at least as directly to Brunswick as to any other company. But it did; that fall Irving was still desperately trying to find a way to slow the smelter development. On August 20, he wrote Boylen (by then president of the company), saying "I, as a shareholder and a director of Brunswick Mining and Smelting feel that the financial risk for the company is too great. A change in the building schedule and different financial arrangements are necessary." In September, he wrote to Gilbert Kerlin, another director, warning him that Brunswick and its shareholders were likely to "get over their heads in debt." Irving believed, he later said, that the company's deteriorating financial condition was due "in large part" to the "many changes, proposed changes, and additions, practically all of which were the result of the premature start of the construction, which meant that the smelter actually was being designed and redesigned during the building programme." The government, on the other hand, thought that Irving himself was responsible for the rising costs.

But that winter came an event that, for a while, pushed Brunswick's problems almost off the stage – so much so that when, in April, a $20,000,000 refinancing of the smelter was undertaken, few people noticed. What happened that November was that the government finally introduced into the legislature the beginnings óf its "Equal Opportunity" program – the program which was to haul New Brunswick society kicking and screaming into the twentieth century.

As always in politics, the fight over the Equal Opportunity program did not take the form of a debate over principles. Principles have to be inferred behind the specific (sometimes apparently silly) issues that people choose to fight on. And, in fact, the principles of Equal Opportunity had been pretty clear for some time before Louis Robichaud introduced the program in the legislature with a long speech on November 16, 1965. They had been enunciated, though somewhat more strictly and toughly, in the report of the Royal Commission – chaired by E.G. Byrne – which had been tabled in the legislature in January 1964; they had been outlined in a government white paper in the spring of 1965. So they were no surprise. Even so, the opposition and the press both clamoured for more detail after the introductory speech. Irving, though, was silent, preoccupied with other matters. He was opposing the projected Saint John Harbour Bridge, which he claimed was too expensive and would probably require prohibitive tolls of his trucks and buses. He was trying to talk the government and Brunswick Mining and Smelting into delaying the smelter construction; he was setting up Bay Steel Corporation. He was sizing up South Nelson Forest Products' Mill, which was for sale because of a recession in Italy that made it impossible for Cartiere del Timavo to retain it. And Irving, an expert at juggling irons into and out of the fire, knew that the real fight over Equal Opportunity would not come until later.

The fall session of the legislature opened quietly enough, with the setting up of a "Law Amendments Committee" to hear citizens' opinions on bills before the legislature and recommend amendments. The committee was the Robichaud government's attempt to demonstrate that it wanted participation in its program, that it would not railroad bills through the legislature. The government even promised that any bill receiving really vociferous and long-lasting opposition in the Law Amendments Committee would be abandoned – a pledge they were later to regret.

Even the introduction of the first few actual bills seemed quiet; the Municipalities Act, and acts surrounding it, such as the soon-to-be-famous Assessment Act, were accepted with only the usual opposition carping. The press was quiet, simply wondering at increasingly frequent intervals what it was all going to cost. But as the deluge of legislation increased, and bill after revolutionary bill poured into the legislature while the government tried to make sense out of New Brunswick's archaic financing, educational, welfare, and justice laws, reactions began to harden, and response to build up. Pressure groups who had been trodden upon began to be heard: the Union of Municipalities called for an immediate general election, for instance (municipalities would be effectively abolished by the Equal Opportunity legislation), and the New Brunswick Teachers' Association screamed at the educational changes embodied in the new laws (teachers were to be upgraded and their salaries equalized across the province). The leader of the opposition, C.B. Sherwood, conducted an inept but widely-reported campaign of nitpicking.

But what was never made clear in any printed public statement was the extent to which the reaction to Equal Opportunity was part of the long tradition of French-English conflict in New Brunswick, a province which had had active chapters of the Ku Klux Klan as late as the thirties. The reaction centred in Fredericton, which claimed that as a municipality it was hard done by in the legislation. But the violence of the public rhetoric and meetings and rallies in the capital city left no doubt of the depth of the hostility to a program which seemed to the Anglophone majority in the St. John River Valley to be stealing from the upstanding Protestant businessmen in order to support an indigent, shiftless French population. The program was widely known (though never in print) as "Evangeline's Revenge".

And, of course, as always in such situations, there was some truth in their perceptions. It was the rich St. John Valley that would be taxed; it was the poor Acadians of Bathurst who stood to gain by a centralization and standardization of education in the province. This accounts, for instance, for the fact that while the provincial Teachers' Association put together a petition condemning the proposed Education Act, the North Shore chapters of the Association almost universally refused to endorse the petition. *They* had nothing to lose in a general levelling.

It was only after bills had received second reading that they could come to the attention of the Law Amendments Committee, with its power to hold public hearings and receive briefs. It soon became apparent that it was in the Law Amendments Committee that the program was going to receive its baptism of fire. Second reading is approval in principle, with room for modification in detail; and it is always in matters of detail that political battles are fought, a lesson that K.C. Irving had learned well indeed.

On December 14 the Law Amendments Committee held its first hearings. The papers announced the hearings with some relish, but raised no expectations of confrontation or drama; presumably all the local pressure groups and offended elements – county governments (which were abolished), school boards (which were to lose their financial power), city governments (which were already agitating for an extension of the time allowed to present briefs to the committee), and Anglophiles, would have a chance to excoriate the legislation, especially the Assessments Act, and the government. No one predicted the spectacular main event in which the centre ring would be occupied by K.C. Irving and the hapless Norbert Theriault, Minister of Municipal Affairs.

The issue? Buried in the Byrne Commission report was a recommendation to abolish municipal tax concessions. A tax concession was an arrangement, designed to lure a business to a specific area, which allowed the business to pay much less than its share of taxes. Normally such a concession would be arranged between a municipality or a county and the business, and then ratified in the form of an act of the legislature. Because of the generally desperate state of New Brunswick's economy, such concessions had been granted widely; and because he held a large proportion of everything in the province, K.C. Irving held a large proportion of those concessions. Almost all his largest firms were receiving such tax breaks: Irving Pulp and Paper, J.D. Irving, Ocean Steel, Brunswick Mining and Smelting, Saint John Shipbuilding and Dry Dock, and the Irving Refinery. And of course the concessions were hefty, since they were meant to provide incentives to already-sizable industries. The $50,000,000 refinery, for instance, paid set taxes moving from $51,500 in 1960 to a projected $75,000 in 1990 – whereas the usual business taxes, at about a dollar and a half per hundred, would bring in ten times that. Even the smallest businesses often enjoyed them: Irving's sawmill in St. Leonard, for instance, had been exempted altogether from municipal taxes for five years in 1962. Altogether, there were seventy-one such concession holders in the province in 1965. Taxed at prevailing rates, the government figured, they would have been worth $3,000,000 a year; in fact, the total tax paid was $1,576,681.

If you consider that Irving held the lion's share of those concessions, and that he knew how good that million and a half dollars must have looked to the financially-troubled government, it's easy to see why any mention of the concessions might strike a sensitive spot in the dinosaur. Irving could ignore a royal commission report, but when someone like Louis Robichaud begins talking about it, you begin to feel it – especially given the growing lack of trust and respect between the two men by 1965.

Thus, when it discovered that Section 3 of Bill 118 included a statement like this, the dinosaur began reacting in earnest:

> ...all provincial, municipal or local taxes or rates on real property shall be calculated and levied upon the whole of the assessment or assessments made under this Act.

It made no difference that the government had said on a number of occasions that it did not intend to revoke already-existent tax concessions, nor that the "Fact Sheet" distributed with the act expressly stated that "the [Royal] Commission's recommendation that existing tax concessions be terminated without compensation was rejected." Even a dinosaur is smart enough to know that no "Fact Sheet" was ever law.

All of this, however, hardly explains the violence of Irving's response to the wording of Section 3 and to the act as a whole. And his reaction was indeed violent, unprecedently so; with a team of advisers, he stormed into the Law Amendments Committee hearings, which had been moved to the floor of the legislature to accomodate the crowds, and attacked the law and the government with language that left no doubt of his contempt for what he called this "breach of faith".

In a scene that members of the legislature would remember vividly years later – in their nightmares, some of them claim – Irving called the act "completely unacceptable", claiming that although Equal Opportunity was all right in principle, "no sane person is going to agree with the method." He went on to charge that the government was trying to "stuff this bill down our throats." Then came the weapon that had always worked before, the threat to apply economic sanctions. "But they should understand that some industries are liable to choke to death. Others," he hinted broadly, "may have to pull back on expansion plans. . . . Surely the province does not expect to attract new industry, or even retain existing industry under such terms. Where are we to place our trust?" No one (especially, it was clear, K.C. Irving), would invest in New Brunswick "in the atmosphere of distrust that this legislation will create."

The crucial element of his argument, however, seems not to have been economic but moral. "As I understand one section of the Assessment Act," he thundered, "the government would assume the power to nullify legitimate tax agreements which have been made by industry. In other words, it wishes to have the authority to destroy agreements, to break faith with companies which have invested millions of dollars on the strength of these very agreements."

What was clearest about Irving's actions was the depth of his distrust of the government, and his fear that if Robichaud got more arbitrary power it would be used against the Irving interests, whatever the government might promise. "In other words, the government may – if it so wishes – grant some industries the right to remain in business while retaining the power – a power morally wrong if not illegally seized – to force other industries out of business. Gentlemen, it is difficult to believe that such legislation could be proposed in New Brunswick."

Difficult indeed.

And no verbal assurances had deterred Irving from reading the act closely and discovering the offending clause. His scepticism about verbal assurances – from any government – was a lesson he had learned in the thirties, when F.C. Manning sneaked in the back door to a bus franchise while Irving stood guard at the front, armed with the verbal assurances of the Saint John Common Council.

The first hearings of the Law Amendments Committee, then, turned out to be one of the longest and stormiest and most curious in the history of legislative committees in New Brunswick. Longest in that it included four sessions, spread over more than twelve hours; stormiest in that not only the Irving interests, but other business organizations, the City of Saint John, the Six Cities organization, and others, all had their say. And curious in that it was not until after all the briefs had been heard, late in the evening, that the hapless Norbert Theriault, who had absorbed (in the absence of Louis Robichaud) the brunt of the attack, rose to explain that Clause 3 had been misconstrued, that the government had never had any intention of revoking the agreements. In a prepared statement delivered late that night (after Robichaud had returned to Fredericton, incidentally), Theriault said that "It is obvious from the statements of many spokesmen here today that there is one misunderstanding that must now be corrected. There is no provision in this act whereby existing tax concession agreements can or will be broken. Nor is there any intention by the government to break any such agreements. The government believes it has a moral obligation to honour those agreements and it fully intends to do so." Theriault said that this had always been government policy, and that the government thought its policy was reflected in the legislation, but promised to revise the provision to make the intention even clearer.

But why did Theriault not speak up until late at night, after twelve hours of acrimonious debate based on a "misunderstanding"? The opposition, the press, and the industrial interests who had presented briefs all asked this question insistently over the next few days, but no convincing answer was ever made public. Theriault's own explanation, the next day, was spectacularly lame: "I felt like getting up after I had heard the first brief, but then I wanted to hear more."

The opposition charged that the government was trying to smuggle in the clause, and intended to revoke the agreements afterwards. Theraiult, they claimed, was silent because what he said at midnight really was a new policy, and he couldn't say it earlier because he couldn't change the policy without talking to Robichaud. The government claimed Clause 3 was there so that industries who wanted "voluntarily" to give up their tax concessions could, but the opposition scoffed at that. Whatever the truth – and members of Robichaud's government still publicly claim they don't know why Theriault was silent – there is no doubt what Irving believed. Once the requisite changes were incorporated in the act, Irving lapsed into his customary quiet, biding his time for an election. The opposition to Equal Opportunity continued to be vociferous, however, particularly in Irving's press. It even continued to cite the revocation of tax concessions as an issue, after the controversial clause had been eliminated; after all, Irving, whom the *Telegraph-Journal* called "the voice of New Brunswick", had accused the Robichaud government of dishonesty. When Irving speaks in New Brunswick the echoes last for years.

The most interesting aspect of Irving's trip to the legislature that December 14, however, is that it was motivated not by business sense, by a nose for political advantage, by economics or by long-range calculation, but by outrage. Irving was indignant. And he was indignant not only at this latest "betrayal", but at what he considered a series of betrayals going back to the Rothesay Paper doublecross, and continuing in 1965 with the government's opposition to his attempts to get control of South Nelson Forest Products, with Louis' insistence about the smelter, with the government's exertion of power in New Brunswick mining generally. But, characteristically, Irving's reaction to all these conflicts was not to sit back and calculate the dollars and cents, but to fight tooth and nail for every inch, to react with anger when confronted and with fury when defeated, to give no quarter and take none. The issue wasn't financial any more: it was moral. Should a good, upstanding, temperate, hard-working Presbyterian allow his hard-won gains to be stolen for the benefit of people who hadn't worked for their gains, who drank, swore, sweated and lied?

Of course not. And the reason Robichaud's compatriots were to remember December 14 in their nightmares was that they knew that, whatever K.C. Irving had said about his lack of involvement in politics, there was no politics in New Brunswick without him. They knew that, from the winter of 1965-66 on, there were two Liberal parties in New Brunswick: the party of K.C. Irving and the party of Louis Robichaud; and that if Louis won the next election it would be the first time that K.C. Irving had lost an election in New Brunswick. There were defections from the cabinet that winter, and prominent Liberals from the St. John Valley repudiated Equal Opportunity.

The battle lines were drawn, and though the skirmishes were not, for the most part, fought in public view, their effects were felt throughout the province. Robichaud had won one when John D. Park, Irving's number one assistant, was fired and turned up at Atlantic Sugar, taking the juicy plum of South Nelson Forest Products with him. Irving won one when he

forced the government to guarantee $50,000,000, sight un-
seen, for Bay Steel, though the government countered by
refusing to proclaim the act incorporating the guarantee until
it had been given a look at the pig through the mouth of the
poke. But these were merely skirmishes. The main forces were
being lined up for two battles: one over Brunswick Mining and
Smelting, and one over the government of the province. This
was a holy war, and casualties were not going to be counted.
That, in the long run, neither side ever really wins such wars;
that usually both sides lose more than they can afford – and
that the population which does the fighting loses everything
– are considerations that do not seem to have entered the
calculations of either side.

Early in 1966 there were rumblings of what was to come;
J.C. ("Charlie") Van Horne, the spectacularly controversial former member of parliament for Restigouche-Madawaska (and,
not quite incidentally, former Irving employee – in positions
including executive assistant – between 1948 and 1955), was
interviewed by phone from California, where he was involved
in real estate. Asked whether it was true that he was coming
back to New Brunswick and an active life in politics, Van
Horne said that while he supported Cy Sherwood as leader of
the Tories, he did feel that more dynamic leadership might be
a good idea, and indicated that he was going to be in New
Brunswick soon "on business" and that he intended to explore
the possibility. Charlie did visit New Bruswick that summer
and fall, and in October, after Sherwood had resigned as leader
and a convention was scheduled for that winter, he visited
Saint John for two days. It does not seem likely that he would
have failed to consult his old employer, K.C. Irving, in a case
like that – and given Irving's developing attitude toward Robichaud's Liberals, it doesn't seem likely that Irving was reluctant to support Van Horne, who said on leaving, "I'm amazed
at the amount of support in Saint John. After being in Saint
John for a couple of days, I was very much impressed." But no
public statements were ever made linking the two, and the
New Brunswick media remained silent on the point. Not so the

national media, which were consistently to describe the situation in the New Brunswick as an Irving-Robichaud showdown.

Charlie Van Horne's campaign for the Tory leadership was an archetype of old-fashioned, medicine-show hucksterism. Treading remorselessly on the toes of the old Tory establishment and its chosen candidate, Richard Hatfield, who advertised himself as the sort of nice boy old ladies like, Van Horne rolled to an overwhelming first-ballot victory at the convention in Fredericton in November, and handily won a conveniently-open seat in the legislature representing his home riding, Restigouche, in February. Charlie's campaign had as main issues his claim that he would win, that "politics is war" – a favourite phrase of his – and that was about all.

During the winter session of the legislature, it became clear that Van Horne did not in fact have much more to offer than hucksterism. If he was indeed Irving's man, the choice proved what Irving himself had always said, that Irving wasn't very interested in politics. Van Horne seemed unable to isolate an issue to campaign on. Rather than attacking the principles of Equal Opportunity, he called it "too little, too late" – hardly a phrase calculated to endear him to the entrenched Neanderthal oppostion to the program. His maiden speech in the legislature betrayed what Robichaud called, accurately, "such an ignorance of New Brunswick politics" that it could "almost be described as a case of indecent exposure." It seemed that Irving's ability to pick men had failed him in the political arena.

In fact, the relationship between Charlie Van Horne and K.C. Irving is one of the mysteries of New Brunswick politics. Their personal styles are as different as they could well be – at least as different as those of Irving and Robichaud. Yet Van Horne worked for Irving for a number of years, part of the time in the intimate capacity of executive assistant: and when he retired from Parliament in 1960, claiming to have accomplished everything he ran for, he had again taken up a business association with Irving. It is difficult to understand how the temperate, quiet, personally restrained and polite Irving could have worked with a man so widely known for his lack of such qualities. Van Horne had, for instance, arrived in Ottawa under the cloud generated by charges that he had been buying votes in New Brunswick. (When a defeated opponent testified that he had seen Charlie offer a constituent a drink from a small bottle, Charlie defended himself with masterly double-entendre: "Knowing my constituents," he said, "I would have lost the election had I insulted anyone of them by offering a drink of liquor from any kind of a *small* bottle.") In his first appearances in the House of Commons, he scandalized parliament with his irresponsible language and conduct, so much so that within a few weeks of his arrival the Speaker of the House had stated that Mr. Van Horne was going to be ignored when he rose to speak; finally, Charlie had to apologize to the House and promise to go straight. But he wasn't good at it, and it soon became known among the Ottawa press corps that Charlie was good for an outrageous statement at almost any hour of the day or night. While in parliament, too, he ordered his restaurant in Campbellton to sell liquor in defiance of the "antiquated" New Brunswick liquor laws, and he crossed party lines to endorse the campaign of Louis Robichaud in 1960 at least partly on the basis of Louis' pledge to do something about those laws.

Though all of this argues that Irving should have been less than overjoyed to have Charlie carrying the ball, there are suggestions that Irving might have been more enthusiastic about him than would seem likely on the surface. In a half-page ad in the *Telegraph-Journal* before the leadership convention, a group of supporters of Van Horne included the following sentence: "One New Brunswick industrialist is quoted in one newspaper as saying: 'Charlie Van Horne is probably the best project organizer in Canada.'" Now, whether or not that "industrialist" was Irving—and how many industrialists does New Brunswick have, after all? – that sort of organizing is a skill Irving does have respect for. Nor is there any doubt that the description is essentially accurate; Charlie Van Horne *can* organize, and his abilities are widely enough known to have involved him in leasing the Place Ville Marie complex in Montreal. And his victory in the leadership race was a triumph of organization, rather than of debate or political acuteness.

The fact that Van Horne could not isolate an issue on which to run his campaign may have impressed Irving a good deal less than the efficient, flamboyant, and effective-looking way in which he employed advertising, the generation of pseudo-events, and other means of manipulating the New Brunswick media. That Irving understood how to win a publicity campaign was made clear not only by his own campaign against the Saint John Harbour Bridge (a campaign which the Fredericton *Gleaner* called "the extraordinary barrage of publicity used by Mr. K.C. Irving") but by the alacrity with which he bought newspapers or radio stations when they came on the market.

In any case, whatever the extent of Irving's support, the stage was now set for what most observers saw as a final showdown over Robichaud's Equal Opportunity program, and as a test of Irving's political influence in New Brunswick. The Robichaud government, at any rate, was ready for an all-out effort. They knew as well as Arthur Irving that K.C. Irving had never lost an election in New Brunswick.

They also knew that Irving had reasons for detestation of the Robichaud regime that weren't yet public, but would be soon. The recurrent conflict over Brunswick Mining and Smelting was about to burst out again.

On the one hand, there were Irving's claims that the rising costs of the smelter were going to break Brunswick, that between unforeseen technical difficulties and a premature start the smelter was a lost cause. By 1967, the smelter, which had once been estimated to cost well under $35,000,000 (construction had actually started at a figure of $20,000,000 was priced at upwards of $70,000,000. The April 1966 refinancing had been insufficient, and East Coast Smelting and Chemical (and its parent, Brunswick itself), was in serious trouble. On the other hand, there was the government, which did not share Irving's opinion about the reason for the castastrophe. They subscribed to M.J. Boylen's theory, that much of the cost was due to the fact that a complex of Irving's companies was in complete control of the physical development of the mine – that, in fact, the longer the concentrator and smelter took and the more expensive they got, the more money Irving made. Not only was Engineering Consultants getting eight per cent of cost, but Irving's companies were supplying the materials for the construction. (Thorne's Hardware, for instance, as a number of people pointed out, was "supplying" items that no hardware wholesaler had ever dealt with before). Boylen's statement was made in the *Northern Miner,* the trade journal of the mining industry, but – not surprisingly – it was never picked up by the New Brunswick papers.

The government, however, knew of it. They took the analysis a step further; if Brunswick actually went bankrupt, only one person was likely to be willing to bail it out: Irving. And, as had been clear from the beginning – what was always clear about him – Irving wanted one hundred per cent. That would mean genuine control; that would mean not having to be responsible to stockholders, to foreign, cautious corporations like Sogemines and Patiño.

In any case, when the government was approached for a further $20,000,000 loan guarantee it refused. Its previous guarantee seemed in some danger already, and to clinch the case, in what seemed increasingly like an election year, the government could not afford to look as though it were channelling public funds into yet another failing industry. If the government was to campaign at least partly on the basis of its successful promotion of industrial growth, it could hardly afford to lose Brunswick at this point, or even to allow it to look as though Brunswick needed to be bailed out. The government's other vaunted achievement, Westmoreland Chemical Park outside Moncton, was also in trouble – was, in fact, to be foreclosed on by the New Brunswick Development Corporation just after the election. Robichaud, therefore, needed Brunswick at almost any cost – even the further (if that were possible) alienation of K.C. Irving.

Through the winter of 1966-67 the government weighed the alternatives as the threat posed by Charlie Van Horne, with Irving behind him, steadily grew. While Charlie was winning his seat in Restigouche, the government was pulling Irving's seat in Brunswick out from under him; on March 18, it was suddenly announced that Noranda Mines, a giant Canadian mining firm with a history of corporate cannibalism, had "appeared" in Brunswick Mining and Smelting; that there had been an emergency loan of $20,000,000 to East Coast Smelting – and then, with its foot in the door and the full, enthusiastic backing of Robichaud and his cabinet, Noranda had arranged to invest $50,000,000 in Brunswick and to take over voting control and management of the huge complex.

When Irving first heard of the proposed deal, he made an arrangement himself to raise the necessary money to bail Brunswick out and to take over voting control himself. At a meeting of the board of directors, before the final arrangement with Noranda, Irving announced that he could make a better deal than Noranda. M.J. Boylen responded, "I thought you'd be up to something," and indicated that both he and Gilbert Kerlin, in spite of Irving's proposal, felt that the Noranda takeover was a good idea. Irving maintains still that his offer was a better one than Noranda's, that his offer involved $63,500,000 and would have kept the management of the vast industry in New Brunswick.

Whether Irving's offer was in fact better or not is one of those questions that will never be answered authoritatively; in situations like this "better" depends on what your ultimate aims are. But it was clear it would not have been better for the Robichaud government. With a Noranda takeover, the government could announce what looked like an endorsement – and an outside endorsement, from a big Upper Canadian company – of their faith in Brunswick. But if the refinancing were to give the mine to Irving, all they could announce was that Brunswick Mining once again had been spared the executioner's axe; there would have been no dramatic changes. And in any case, by this time the government had come to believe that much of the problem with the smelter was due to Irving's management.

148

One of the government's men on the board of directors was, astonishingly enough, E.G. Byrne, the main author of the Bryne Commission Report. Byrne made the government's position crystal clear: unless Irving were out, there'd be no more government assistance in Brunswick's affairs. Given the state of affairs, the board of directors had no choice. Even Irving himself, at a June stockholder's meeting to verify the board's decision, admitted that there was no alternative to voting for the Noranda takeover. With the shareholder's approval, then, what happened was that Noranda bought 100,000 newly-created $5.00 preferred shares, and $49,500,000 in bonds, the bonds being convertible into 10,000,000 Brunswick common shares. The total investment then, was $50,000,000, of which Brunswick immediately used $33,000,000 to retire outstanding debts, retaining $17,000,000 in new capital funds. After the deal, Noranda (potentially) owned fifty-one per cent of Brunswick's shares and was assigned the powers of management that had previously been held by Irving's Engineering Consultants Limited, holder of $8,000,000 worth of Brunswick bonds (which were bought back by the company with Noranda's money). The reason Noranda bought bonds rather than shares was that Noranda was minimizing its risk – hedging its bets, a tactic Irving undoubtedly would not have employed. With bonds, if the company failed, Noranda would be one of the creditors and might recover something; with shares, if the company failed, Noranda would participate in the failure and lose whatever the company lost.

After the dust settled – if, in fact, it ever settled completely – Noranda had potential voting control, with a majority interest, eight new seats on an expanded fifteen man board of directors, and their own president, W.S. Row. Boylen's company, First Maritime Mining, held a twenty-three per cent interest, Patiño held eleven per cent, and Irving, through various subsidiaires like Kent Lines, Key Anacon Mines, and so forth, owned thirteen per cent. And it looked as though Robichaud and company had won: on March 16, the Minister of Finance, W.G. DesBrisay, announced what sounded to a casual listener like a financial breakthrough. Another huge company was investing its money and expertise in the development of "New Brunswick's vast mineral resources." "In our judgement," DesBrisay said, "this agreement is good for New Brunswick. It is in every way good for the province." If he seemed to protest a little too much, few Liberals seemed to notice. Nor was much made of the government's role in Brunswick's financial troubles, though the *Northern Miner* did say that the story that came out at the stockholders' meeting was "that a beleaguered company had severely overextended itself and was coerced into extraordinary financial commitments through political pressure for construction of a smelter in New Brunswick." And though at the meeting E.R.E. Carter, the Patiño executive who had been president of Brunswick, said that *he* couldn't "recall the company being forced into the smelter project by government pressure," Irving made no bones about it: the premier had told them to go ahead with the smelter "or somebody else would." "I realized the danger of going ahead without the money," Irving said after the stockholders' meeting. "The premier said, no, go ahead. . . . I am unhappy with what has taken place and at what is taking place."

If there ever was a clear example of the differences between the way Irving companies operate and the way other businesses do, it lies in the aftermath of this takeover. It can be seen not only in the reaction of the Irving interests to losing – a reaction that was loud, public, litigious and vindictive (beginning after the stockholders' meeting, continuing through scores of lawsuits, of which the first were filed in October, and climaxing in the spectacular Brunswick stockholders' meetings of 1969-71, when Irving and his interests contested everything the new management was doing), but also in the kinds of management decisions that characterized the company before and after Irving lost control.

Just previous to the takeover, for instance, the company was planning to invest about $4,000,000 in the development of a deepwater port at Belledune – on the assumption, first, that the fertilizer and chemical industries were going to go, and second, that the multiplier effect would bring the economy of the whole area to life, justifying the port and making it, in the long haul, an economically justifiable proposition. After the takeover, on the other hand, Noranda decided not to go ahead with the port. At the 1970 stockholders' meeting, when the Irving entourage accused them of slackness, W.S. Row said, "Sure it could have been a nice development, but to serve what purpose? It could well have been a white elephant." A cost accounting decision. Sophisticated, conservative management. Irving called the action "an unbelievable blunder", and went on, "had the east breakwater been built, other wharves would have been in existence today." All Brunswick had to do, he maintained, was wait; once the breakwater was in, the development would almost take care of itself.

And that's the difference. As Irving has said many times, if you go public you can't take the calculated risk. If you're not a New Brunswicker, you don't believe in New Brunswick's potential to develop around your seeds. And, most important, if you keep expanding, the future will look out for itself.

But the long term consequences of moving the management of Brunswick out of the province, and into the hands of conventional businessmen, was not the sort of issue you could make any political hay out of – certainly not in New Brunswick in 1967, and in the face of a government whose political skills had already claimed the issue as their own by publicizing the Noranda takeover as an expansion, as a sign of vigorous growth. And it was most certainly not the kind of issue that a Charlie Van Horne could capitalize on.

In fact, there did not seem to be many issues of the kind that Van Horne was comfortable with. Though the pressure of the campaign which developed in the fall was heavy, the content was almost nil. Van Horne neither capitalized consistently on the anti-French component of the Equal Opportunity opposition, nor mounted a reasoned attack on the program. He posed no solutions and offered no clearly alternate position. His platform proposed a singularly vague "crash program" to help New Brunswick, a pitch to Ottawa for more money, and a 113-point manifesto which Louis consistently burlesqued at Liberal rallies, holding a six-foot roll of newspaper clippings over his head, letting it slowly unfurl, and announcing "this is the Conservative platform." It seems to have been the Van Horne strategy to commit himself to nothing, but simply to capitalize on the strong anti-Robichaud feeling. As the campaign wore on, however, and the Liberals refused to panic, Van Horne took to a fair amount of personal attack on Louis Robichaud – a tactic which damaged both sides.

But the most astonishing thing about the campaign was the public invisibility of the main figure. It was openly known among New Brunswick politicians and in the media in the rest of Canada that it was K.C. Irving who had brought Van Horne back from California; but Irving's name was never mentioned in the papers during the campaign in connection with Van Horne. Even on the occasions, late in the campaign, when Robichaud would refer to "the interests which brought Van Horne back and financed this campaign" or to certain unnamed parties who wanted to run New Brunswick without standing for election, the newspapers failed to report the references. As far as the average New Brunswicker knew, Irving stood as aloof from this campaign as he claimed always to stand from any kind of politics. Why either side did not make more of an issue of Van Horne's connection with Irving is hard to understand except on the hypothesis that neither could predict the effect with any certainty. Would the voters react to the situation by rejecting Van Horne as "Irving's pawn", or would they – as the letters in the papers have always suggested they might – accept whatever Irving decided as probably good for New Brunswick? Either way, the introduction of that name into the campaign never happened, even though Robichaud himself clearly believed in the later stages of the campaign that it was an act that would finish off Van Horne.

Whether he was right or not, it turned out not to be necessary. Irving's silence intact, the headlines in the *Telegraph-Journal* on the morning of November 24 read "Liberals Win Cliff-Hanger – Van Horne Loses His Seat." Robichaud had survived, and for the first time, ever, Irving had lost a New Brunswick election. But the victory was, finally, a hollow one. Though the government lasted three years more, somehow the election and the panic about Irving's opposition had sapped much of its strength and a lot of its support, and in the years after 1967 it never attained the activity of the earlier period. The government became a caretaker of Equal Opportunity, an implementer, and increasingly less popular. As Senator Charles McElman, long-time adviser to Robichaud, was later to say, "Just as we beat the Conservatives in 1956, so they beat us in 1967. In both cases the election that actually turned the power over was an anticlimax". After 1967, he says, "the tarnish was on" the Liberal government. So in one sense – the sense that it was his money and support which made Van Horne's campaign not only possible but formidable – it was not actually a loss for Irving. The principle remained: cross Irving and your political life is in danger. Every politician in New Brunswick knew the power that had been brought to bear during that election. The next government to be elected in New Brunswick would be at least as reluctant to oppose the Irving interests as the Robichaud government had been when it was elected.

Both sides, then, lost the 1967 election. And so did the people – the dispossessed Acadians, the pulp cutters on the back roads of central New Brunswick, the fishermen – who stood to benefit by a further, imaginative development of the Equal Opportunity program. It would be a long time before a government laid its future on the line by trying to tax the English businessman to pay for social development among the dispossessed, even in as tentative and hesitant a way as the Robichaud government had.

Equally, both sides lost the fight over Brunswick Mining and Smelting. Irving lost control of the richest mineral lode in Canada, and of the sort of industrial development that might proceed from that lode. The Robichaud government never did get its smelter, never did get to say that it had awakened the economy of the North Shore. And it had to allow control of the corporation to slip away to Toronto and the board rooms of Upper Canada, where a company like Noranda Mines (safely insulated from the consequences) would make the decisions about whether the town of Bathurst starved or flourished. And of course the poor Acadians lost, as their economy lapsed again into its broken and uneasy slumber.

But the one thing everyone in the province knew was that you can never count the dinosaur out altogether. Almost as soon as Noranda was firmly in control, the stock of companies like Key Anacon Mines, First Maritimes Mining, and other Brunswick stockholders began to be gobbled up by companies like K.C. Irving Ltd. and Barclay's (Nassau) Nominees Ltd. (Nassau? Isn't that where Irving went when he left the province?) And everyone knew that when – and if – Noranda tired of coping with the disastered smelter, with the pressure of lawsuits and general harassment from Irving companies, with the importunities of frightened and hungry governments, the dinosaur would still be there, patiently waiting. Dinosaurs have lots of time.

CHAPTER FIVE

The Voice of New Brunswick

The most publicized segment of the Irving empire is the monopoly of the media in New Brunswick. Since the 1969 attack on his media empire in the Senate by former Louis Robichaud aide Senator Charles McElman, the Combines Branch investigation which began shortly thereafter, and more particularly since the Special Senate Mass Media Committee hearings in the spring of 1970, the publication of their three-volume report the following winter, and the prosecution of the Irving interests under the Combines Act in the winter of 1972-73, there is hardly anyone in the country who isn't aware that the Irving dinosaur owns all five English language daily newspapers in New Brunswick. Or that it owns the largest of the four radio stations in Saint John (and the only TV station – one of two in the province). Or that Irving's television station is broadcast into 94.9 per cent of the TV sets in the province. Or that, for long periods of time, the ownership of that vast proportion of New Brunswick's media was kept completely secret from the public.

Because of all that publicity, many of the more spectacular abuses of the public trust which have resulted from the Irving media monopoly are also now well known. The way in which the papers have shied away from any meaningful investigation of industrial pollution in New Brunswick, for instance; the long-standing conspiracy of silence about Irving's business dealings; the media's secrecy about its own ownership; and the astonishing way the papers treat Irving as what the *Telegraph-Journal* once called him – the voice of New Brunswick – all have become part of Canada's common stock of knowledge.

Much of that publicity is, almost singlehandedly, the work of a New Brunswick Liberal Senator named Charles McElman. In some ways the struggle over the media of New Brunswick represents another round in the struggle between Irving interests and the Robichaud government, represented in this round by Senator McElman, who was a very central figure in the fight over the Equal Opportunity program, and sat for a time on the board of Brunswick Mining and Smelting as the government representative. He spent, in other words, most of the early sixties in the thick of the fight over Brunswick, Equal Opportunity, industrial tax concessions and pulpwood. It was in that fight, he says, that he learned not only how thoroughly the newspapers were under Irving's thumb, but also how important their position could be in a political struggle.

But the examples he brought to the attention of the Senate – and ultimately of the nation – ranged well beyond the political. It was Senator McElman, for instance, who recounted the story of the explosion and fire in the crew's quarters aboard the oil tanker MV *Irvingstream* in Saint John harbour, and pointed to the *Telegraph-Journal* laying the cause of the grim accident at the door of the federal government – which, it said editorially, did not provide sufficient fireboats. It said so even though its own story admitted that the fire chief said that fireboats were not a factor. And when the inquest accused the company of negligence, there was no editorial mention of it in the paper. As far as the casual reader knew, five men had died because Ottawa didn't provide fireboats.

But perhaps McElman's most spectacular example of journalistic malfeasance involved the senator personally. On March 10 and 11, 1971, he made a long, well-documented speech in the Senate attacking, once again, the Irving monopoly in New Brunswick. Reaffirming his admiration for K.C. Irving himself, McElman told the story of the *Irvingstream*, pointed out the deep secrecy surrounding Irving's acquisition of the Fredericton *Gleaner* (the president of New Brunswick Broadcasting Limited, a close associate of Irving, didn't even know of it), and cited some instances in the long history of editorial silence about Irving companies.

When the Senate recessed on March 10, the Canadian Press filed a story immediately. The story was carried the next morning by the Moncton *Times,* along with an editorial calling on McElman either to show real abuses or shut up – apparently having read neither McElman's speech nor the Davey Mass Media Committee report. But it was the *Telegraph-Journal* that handled McElman's speech most spectacularly. On the same day that the story made the front page of the *Times* there wasn't a word about it in the *Telegraph-Journal.* And since both are morning papers and go to press at the same time, it wasn't because they hadn't received the CP dispatch in time. The next day's front page made it clear why the story hadn't been published. The March 12 headline ran: "McElman Continues Attack: 'Alley Cat' Charge Levelled in Senate," and another front page story was headed "Venemous . . . Garbage . . . Scurrilous . . . MPs React to McElman Charges." Richard Jackson, an Ottawa journalist whose uninspired syndicated column is the *Telegraph-Journal*'s only contact with Ottawa, had apparently run out and garnered comments from all the old dependable pro-Irving, anti-Robichaud and McElman M.P.s and senators in Ottawa. Saint John-Lancaster Tory M.P. Tom Bell, whose family are Irving business associates, called the speech "venemous" and "cowardly". Senator David Walker, an old personal friend of Brigadier Wardell, who had been attacked by McElman's speech, said "this has been a filthy afternoon" and – in Jackson's phrase – "twitted" McElman about having been Robichaud's private secretary. Robert Coates, a Nova Scotia Tory whose flatulent book about the ouster of John Diefenbaker as party leader had been published and puffed by Wardell, called McElman's speech "the most reprehensible action that I have known in my fourteen years as a Member of Parliament." (Easily shocked, these politicians.) With his customary precision, former New Brunswick Conservative premier and Diefenbaker cabinet member Hugh John Flemming said that Wardell had made "a definite and most oustanding contribution" and "an unusual and most definite contribution."

That was the front page. On page four, the editorial was headed "A Filthy Afternoon"; and opposite was another reprinting of Walker's comment, in a box; above that Wardell's reply; and above that the original CP story.

It is hard to believe that in the course of defending itself against a charge of manipulating the news a newspaper could manipulate the news so blatantly. A satirist who created such an irony would be accused of exaggeration.

There are, of course, other equally well-known instances of news manipulating: the distortion of Laurier LaPierre's speech, at Memramcook, near Moncton, in 1969, through which a hard-hitting socialist attack on Irving and his ilk became an argument against Maritime Union, for instance; the consolidated push by the Saint John media behind Irving's attempt to modify the plan for the Saint John Harbour Bridge in 1965; the elaborately orchestrated announcement of Irving's plans for expanding the Brunswick Mining and Smelting complex in Bathurst in October of 1964; what McElman called the "indecent burial" of a story involving pollution from the Irving mill in Saint John; the near-impossibility of obtaining coverage of labour troubles involving Irving in the forties and fifties.

It is difficult to believe – much less to prove in a court of law – that such incidents are the results of conspiracy, that the news has been distorted at the behest of K.C. Irving's financial interests. A lot of different and complex and subtle elements are involved in an editor's decision about how to handle a story or what sort of headline to put on it. It is next to impossible to locate the specific determinant that, for instance, indecently buried on an inside page a consultant's report accusing the

Irving pulp mill of dumping 27,000,000 gallons of waste a day into Saint John harbour. Senator McElman inferred, when he described the situation on the Senate floor, that it was a measure to protect the Irving companies from adverse publicity. But the management of the paper said that the decision was taken because the story had already been on the front page of the previous evening's *Times-Globe.* But who can know what was in the editor's mind that night as he set up the morning *Telegraph-Journal?* The only thing we can be certain of is that he did *not* phone the management of the pulp mill. In any such case there are similar complications. Maybe the papers *did* see the logic of Irving's objections to the location of the New Harbour Bridge; maybe Laurier LaPierre's speech *was* misrepresented merely because of laziness or ineptitude; maybe all the media in New Brunswick *did* agree on the importance of the Brunswick Mining announcement and agree to treat it the same way because it was convenient. Maybe labour's point of view just *didn't* make much sense to the newspapers in the forties. Maybe.

And, indeed, it is most certain that you can find independent newspapers making similar decisions and operating on similar assumptions, just as the Irving papers have made similar decisions about non-Irving companies. The *Telegraph-Journal* has never crusaded against Irving's lavish tax concessions or unabated pollution, to be sure; but then they've never had much to say about those of Consolidated-Bathurst or the Fraser Companies either.

There is yet a worse complication in any attempt to demonstrate the evil of monopoly ownership of the media. Clear, concrete examples like these may be the most striking ones there are, but they are far from the most serious and potentially dangerous ways in which the news can be manipulated. The most crucial decisions are made much earlier in the process: decisions not to cover a story, and more especially decisions not to investigate some area likely to yield a story. And such decisions are, of course, in many cases not decisions at all; often the alternatives are never considered. It is very rare, for example, to find a case like the one cited by journalist Donald Cameron in his testimony before the Davey committee, in which the Fredericton *Gleaner's* investigation of welfare abuses was never printed because the favourable results of the investigation conflicted with the paper's policy. More often, the paper simply never notices an area to be investigated. Thus none of the New Brunswick media have done a study of the economics of the pulp and paper industry and its relationship with the pulp cutter and small woodlot owner. And this is not because they have been told by their owner, K.C. Irving Limited, to stay away from the subject; it is rather because they don't see that such a study needs to be done, that there are flagrant abuses waiting to be discovered. Whether, in turn, this is because they are lazy and unimaginative or because they perceive clearly where their fundamental interest lies can't be said for sure – not even by the people directly responsible.

A case which is not quite so ambiguous represents the papers' coverage of areas directly involving Irving. An inspection, for instance, of the Irving press in the period between his spectacular trip to the provincial legislature in December 1965, and the election seventeen months later, reveals no mention at all of Irving's political position, of his involvement in the campaign, even of his attitudes toward the on-going implementaton of the Equal Opportunity program. At the same time, the national media were making it perfectly clear that it was Irving who was behind the Van Horne campaign. But their inferences were, by and large, made from a distance; the local media maintained complete silence on the subject. Even the fact that Van Horne had once been K.C. Irving's executive assistant was never mentioned in the Irving press. In such a case, of course, it is as difficult to ascertain direct influence as in any other; but the conflict of interest is much easier to see. Any sceptical, tough-minded and aggressive journalism would have come into direct conflict with the interests of the management of the papers. Whether there ever actually was an order at the *Telegraph-Journal* that Irving's name was never to be mentioned in print without getting clearance from the publisher, there were most certainly reporters who believed there was.

An even more subtle distortion occurs when newspapers report news events only in isolation, making no connection between them for their readership. In July 1970 *The Mysterious East* published a story showing that the chairman of the New Brunswick Water Authority, the governmental organization charged with enforcing the province's anti-pollution laws, had also (simultaneously) been the Executive Secretary of the New Brunswick Forest Products Association, an organization of pulp and paper businesses (the province's largest water polluters) set up to represent the industry in any dealings with government. The Davey Commission report called the story "an astonishing scoop", which should have been "joyously trumpeted" by the daily papers of the region – but wasn't. The report went on, "The uncharitable might be led to suspect that this lack of journalistic enterprise was connected to the fact that K.C. Irving, owner of one of the province's largest pulp mills, also owns all five New Brunswick English-language dailies." On December 10, Michael Wardell ran a hysterical, two-full-column editorial response to the Davey report, in the course of which he defended the *Gleaner*'s ignoring of the story: "Some of the biographical material in the article was available in the files of the *Daily Cleaner* as far back as October, 1958."

Even assuming that Wardell means to say that the paper had printed the material, not merely held it in its files, there is a wealth of insight into the editorial process in that statement; it implies that if the paper has printed the facts, it has no obligation to connect them. On one occasion, you mention a man's association with the pulp and paper industry; on another his appointment to a government agency. For the *Gleaner* – and newspapers like it – that's your obligation, your upholding of a public trust. The fact that the two facts are nearly meaningless in isolation, that the story lies in their connection, is surely outside your ken, isn't it?

Or take the story of the *Irving Whale*. When the oil barge

sank in the Gulf of St. Lawrence on Monday, September 7, 1970, the Irving papers faithfully reported all the details about its 3,500-ton cargo of bunker "C" oil, its ownership and location, the statements of Irving himself and Irving officials, government spokesmen, and all the customary appurtenances of news reporting. None, however, made any reference to the *Irving Whale's* previous history. No one mentioned that the *Irving Whale* had been rented (at $1,000 a day) to the task force cleaning up after the Liberian tanker *Arrow* spilled 3,800,000 gallons of bunker "C" oil in Chedabucto Bay. Or that at that time P.D. McTaggart-Cowan had said that the barge "was in terrible shape – dirty, with the safety rails half off over the bow," and that the barge had been a good vessel when built in 1966, but "it didn't look as if it had had any maintenance since." Nor did they make much of the fact that the *Whale* had spilled 3,000 gallons of bunker oil near Newfoundland's Burin Peninsula only months before. Even the comment by a Transport Department official that the barge was "very, very heavily loaded" just prior to its sinking was buried at the end of a story outlining the Transport Minister's new, tougher anti-pollution policy. The clear implications created by the juxtaposition of these facts – of callous irresponsibility toward the environment, of carelessness and probably negligence – remained entirely absent from the newspaper accounts of the events. Yet the press could say in all truthfulness that it had not suppressed any of the news, that it had printed all the facts.

And here again it is almost impossible to distinguish between mere laziness and suppression. Indeed, Donald Cameron made the point, in a CBC program on the Maritime press, that if you want to create a conservative, status quo, pro-establishment press, the best way to do it is simply to hire the incompetent. Incompetent journalism is better for the dinosaurs than journalism which is committed to their cause. Finally, then, perhaps the most convincing argument against press monopolies like that of Irving is that since incompetence is so attractive, both ideologically and financially, the monopoly will almost by nature create an incompetent press. Of course, as was demonstrated by the independent Fredericton *Gleaner* under Brigadier Wardell, and even more so under its previous ownership, monopoly is not the only cause of incompetent journalism. A small readership and consequent low advertising rates and lack of money; inexperience; an excess of experience leading to boredom; and misguided notions as to what journalism ought to do for society can all lead to the growth of what the Davey report called a "journalistic disaster area". Whether or not, then, it is the ownership of the newspapers that has produced that situation is an immense and complex question. But as long as the media in New Brunswick are controlled by one financial interest, there is no chance whatsoever that it is going to improve very noticeably. Good journalism is contrary to the interests of such entities; as the Davey Committee insists in its report, the job of journalism is to prepare people for social change. And if you're doing as well under the present system as the Irving dinosaur is, social change – of whatever kind – must look like a threat. Dinosaurs do not adapt to change.

Whether the dinosaur consciously knew what it was doing when it devoured the newspapers and the radio and television stations, or whether it simply acted according to instinct, is another difficult and complex question. Irving himself testified before the Davey Committee that it was merely a matter of business instinct. Asked by Yves Fortier whether he bought anything that was for sale, Irving answered, "If it is a reasonable buy and providing I have the money."

"When you are dealing, do you treat the acquisition of newspapers any differently than you treat the acquisition of other commodities?"

"Well, I don't," Irving replied. "You have to select your commodities."

"Well, I think it is for you to do that."

"All right." Irving was, in Senator McElman's words, "testy" at this point; he does not like being badgered. "So far as a good commodity itself, I deal with all good commodities and I put the newspaper business in the same category."

This is, to be sure, a somewhat casual attitude to hold about the public trust involved in newspaper ownership. As Senator McElman commented later, it is enough to "chill the printer's ink" in a good reporter's veins. But it still does not decide the extent to which the media empire was assembled knowingly and deliberately as a monopoly of information in New Brunswick. For Irving never explained why the newspapers were an attractive commodity; and he did make abundantly clear that whatever the reason for their attractiveness, it was not primarily financial.

Like so many other questions about the motives of dinosaurs, it seems that this one can only be answered by looking at its specific actions. The important questions, then, are not concerned with what Irving and his executives *say* about the reasons for their actions, but rather with precisely what their actions *were*. How, in fact, did the Irving interests come to have such an unprecedented level of control over the channels of public information in New Brunswick – and to what uses has that control been put?

Like so many of Irving's industrial and economic structures, the media empire began, and still has its cornerstone, in Saint John. The Saint John newspapers were the first to be purchased, and remain the largest and most influential newspapers in the province. In effect, they are only one newspaper; the morning *Telegraph-Journal* (the only newspaper in the province with pretensions to cover all of New Brunswick) and the evening *Times-Globe* are sister papers, sharing offices, staff, management and editorial policy.

It was not always so. During the last half of the nineteenth century, a dozen different papers competed, at varying times, for the small Saint John readership. The *Morning Globe*, for instance, established in 1858, became the *Evening Globe* in 1859, absorbed *The Colonial Empire* in 1863 and became the *Saint John Globe* in 1867, which it remained until 1927, when it joined *The Evening Times and The Star* (which represented a 1910 amalgamation of two previous papers) and became known as the *Evening Times-Globe*. A similar evolution characterized the morning paper, which began as the *Daily Tele-graph* in 1864, became the *Morning Journal* in 1865 and *The Saint John Daily Telegraph and Morning Journal* in 1869, four years later contracting its name to *The Daily Telegraph*. It absorbed the thirty-year old *Saint John Daily Sun* in 1910. At the same time a group of Conservatives from Fredericton founded a paper called *The Standard,* which became the *Saint John Standard* and then, in 1922, the *Daily Journal.* In 1923 that paper merged with the *Daily Telegraph and the Sun* to form the *Saint John Telegraph-Journal.*

The final stages of this process of merger and consolidation were performed by Howard P. Robinson, the scion of a Sussex, New Brunswick, publishing family who rose to become, in the early twentieth century, a figure almost as dominant as K.C. Irving was to be in the middle years of the century. Almost the single-handed promoter of the New Brunswick Telephone Company, Robinson in the late thirties and forties was a direc-tor of the Royal Bank and of the C.P.R.; chairman of the board of New Brunswick Telephone; and primary figure in The New Brunswick Publishing Company, which he created. In June of 1923 the company was set up; in July it acquired and merged the *Daily Telegraph* and the *Daily Journal;* and in 1927 it acquired and merged the two papers which became the *Times-Globe.* Robinson, a major force in the Saint John business com-munity, thus became and remained the dominant voice in Saint John for over twenty years. There was, that is to say, plenty of precedent for Irving's assembling a media monopoly in New Brunswick. When he arrived in Saint John in 1930, the newspapers were all safely under one roof. And four years later, New Brunswick Broadcasting Limited, an offspring of Robinson's New Brunswick Publishing, took over the city's only radio station, further consolidating control of the public sources of information.

Irving's aquisition of control of New Brunswick Publishing was, then, hardly a break with tradition. At the time few peo-ple knew that New Brunswick Publishing was reorganized in December 1944 and that shortly thereafter Robinson's interest passed to Irving; and those who did made no claims to know the motives of either party to the deal. But hindsight suggests a passing on of a torch; if H.P. Robinson was to Saint John in 1940 what Irving was to be to New Brunswick in 1960, it is clear that Irving succeeded to Robinson's position between 1945, when he bought the newspapers, and June 1949, when he bought the elegant white mansion at 197 Mount Pleasant Avenue in Saint John that had been a focal point of Saint John business activity for years, Robinson's house. Robinson, retiring from business, it seems clear, was passing on his position of primacy in Saint John business to the younger man.

And, whatever Irving's conscious motives, the control of the media in Saint John was at least as attractive a proposition as the control of that of the whole province was to be a few years later. Increasingly involved in public affairs and in dealings with the government, Irving could hardly have been unaware of the sort of potential involved in media ownership – potential that he was later to realize in the final rounds of the bus franchise struggle.

And when, three and a half years later, Moncton Publishers Limited began to look shaky, Irving formed Moncton Publishing and bought the two Moncton papers through it. At that point he controlled the papers in the only sizable population and financial centres in New Brunswick. The only English-language daily newspaper left was the Fredericton *Gleaner;* and even though it was the provincial capital, Fredericton was still a very small town. Moreover, then as now, more Frederictonians read the Saint John *Telegraph-Journal* as a major news source than read this local paper.

When, in 1951, University Press Limited, set up by the recently-arrived Beaverbrook associate, Michael Wardell, took over the Fredericton *Gleaner,* it became certain that no anti-Irving voice would be raised in New Brunswick; Wardell unashamedly worshipped Irving and his works and for the next twenty years the most consistently and openly pro-Irving voices in the province were to be his *Gleaner* and the associated magazine, the *Atlantic Advocate.* It was not until

1968, with Wardell ready to retire back to his native England, that Irving felt it necessary to acquire control of University Press, and complete in economic terms the dominance that had existed in *de facto* terms for two decades.

The degree of secrecy surrounding Irving's assemblage of his newspaper empire is significant; the dinosaur was clearly aware that its appetite was moving beyond bounds. Of course, all of Irving's business is conducted, as far as possible, out of public view. That is a major reason for his desire to gain complete ownership, rather than effective control, of business. And there are a number of readily understandable motives for secrecy in this case: not only the apprehension that an anti-monopoly proceeding might be launched, but also the perception that if the public was widely aware that Irving interests owned the newspapers, value of their support would be markedly lessened. In any case, throughout the late fifties and early sixties, journalists reported no more than that "it was rumoured" that Irving controlled four of the province's newspapers. Clear public confirmation was never offered. Research might have established the fact, but none was done. It was not until after Irving had absorbed the *Gleaner* that knowledge of the ownership of the media became widespread. And that transaction became public in a very roundabout way.

The deal by which Irving took over ownership of University Press was consummated on May 15, 1968. The degree of secrecy involved can perhaps best be seen by considering that not only the general public, but the *Gleaner* staff and management, and many of Irving's close associates, were kept in the dark. L.F. Daley, a Halifax attorney who had been president of New Brunswick Broadcasting since 1962 and one of Irving's principal legal advisers, testified before the C.R.T.C. the following November that as far as he knew there was no connection between the *Gleaner* and the Irving papers in Saint John and Moncton. Rumours of an Irving interest in the *Gleaner* had been circulating for years – hence the C.R.T.C.'s question – and Daley's testimony served to quiet them measurably.

Months later, however, Senator McElman heard, in England and from an associate of Michael Wardell, that Wardell had sold his interest in the *Gleaner* to Irving. On March 11, 1969, he announced in the Senate that the Irving media monopoly was now complete, and within days he had made a formal request to the Combines Branch of the Consumers Affairs Department to investigate the Irving group. The furor stirred up by his announcement, and his subsequent request to the Combines Branch, was considerable.

On Wednesday, the following day, the *Gleaner* ran a Canadian Press story on McElman's speech, putting it on the inside of page two, with the obituaries and below the weather forecast. The next day, however, there was a story on the front page headed "Control of the *Daily Gleaner*", with a boldface lead which ran, "Today a change in the relative holdings of the shareholders of the company owning the *Daily Gleaner* is announced." Under that there were two stories – "Irving issues Statement" and "Wardell remains Publisher." None of the stories acknowledged that the announcement was of an event that had taken place almost a year before, or that the only reason it was being announced now was that McElman had taken the cat that Wardell had let out of the bag and tossed it onto the Senate floor. Wardell's statement, in full, ran like this: "Mr. Irving some months ago became a major shareholder in the company which controls the *Daily Gleaner.* For the good of the province and in the interests of the staff of the *Gleaner*, to retain control within the province as well as to safeguard my own interests, I invited Mr. Irving to acquire this interest in the company. I still have a substantial shareholding and I continue to exercise control of policy and full direction of the newspaper, with the help of a fine and efficient staff." An equally unrevealing lead editorial, less than a hundred words in length, said the change had "no relevance to the services which the *Daily Gleaner* will continue to provide for its readers, or to the policy of its editorial column." The attempt to make the deal seem nothing more than a minor financial reorganization seems, by hindsight, to be disingenuous at the least. It is difficult to believe that Wardell had no idea at all that within a little more than a year the *Gleaner* would have a new publisher and he would be on his way back to England to retire. Moreover, there were persistent rumours that Southam Press had made a higher offer than Irving for the *Gleaner,* a fact which, if true, suggests someone was thinking in terms of a deal more far-reaching than merely a minor financial readjustment.

Irving's statement was equally interesting. "There is nothing secret about it," he said. The whole deal was described in a brief submitted to the C.R.T.C., and "the information will be public this week if the C.R.T.C. wishes to make it public or, at the latest, at the time of the next hearing." He could, he said, only presume that McElman knew the information was to be made public and made his own announcement first so that he could claim the deal was a "secret". He suggested McElman's motives were personal pique, stated that he did not feel that his ownership of the media was something to be apologized for, asserted his own lack of involvement in the newspapers' operations, and cited as an example the fact that Brigadier Wardell had retained control of the *Gleaner.* "Senator McElman," he concluded, "has implied that there is something wrong with New Brunswickers owning and building businesses in New Brunswick. I don't agree with him." He was unlimbering the most trusty weapon in his armoury. "I have spent my whole life working in New Brunswick and I don't think New Brunswickers have to turn any enterprise over to outsiders. Does Senator McElman also believe that Canada would be better served if the news media were foreign owned and controlled? I have had many opportunities to sell the newspaper properties over the years, but it has been my view that they should be operated by New Brunswickers, not by some company with a head office in Toronto or some foreign country."

In a limited way, the tactic worked again, as the letters columns filled with defenses of Irving and attacks on his opponents. But this time the situation was different, for the forces set at work by McElman were outside Irving's scope. D.H.W.

Henry, the Director of Investigation and Research under the Combines Act, had already instituted an investigation. Moreover, within a week, on March 18, the creation of a Special Senate Committee on Mass Media was finally approved by the Senate. Originating as they did outside New Brunswick, the two new forces created an entirely new arena for the fight, drawing national attention to the New Brunswick media situation and indirectly to the problem of the economic dominance of New Brunswick by one corporation. But with the wheels of justice grinding as slowly as they ever do, it was to be some time before any effects were felt.

Publicity generated by the Combines Branch investigation was to be sporadic and general, drawing attention to the fact of the investigation but not to the details. The ensuing October, for instance, it was widely reported that investigators from the Combines Branch had searched the offices of New Brunswick Publishing, Moncton Publishing, University Press, K.C. Irving Limited, and the homes of Wardell, Irving, and Ralph Costello, Irving's lieutenant and the principal figure in the Moncton and Saint John publishing and broadcasting companies. Most of the publicity surrounding this event was due to the screams of anguished protest loosed by Michael Wardell, who termed the action a "raid" by a "vice squad" which treated him as though he were a member of the Mafia, and generally managed to create the impression that his door had been broken down by storm troopers. That Wardell's response was somewhat excessive became clear in January, when the Toronto *Star* ran a picture of the attractive young brunette who had led the "vice squad" and who was present when D.H.W. Henry described their search to the Davey Committee. Such publicity drew attention to the fact that there was a problem in New Brunswick, but did not do much to clarify its nature.

The Davey Committee was another matter. One of its central concerns – as might have been expected, since McElman's initiative was a major factor in its formation – was the New Brunswick situation. Dalton Camp, in fact, said to the Committee that "as a Maritimer I have been interested in the Committee's close examination of media in New Brunswick. For a time, I suspected that the Committee might not have any other purpose." It is interesting, too, that Ralph Costello was the first witness to appear before the Committee when it opened its hearings on December 9 – though he appeared not in his capacity as central figure in the Irving media empire, but as President of the Canadian Daily Newspaper Publishers' Association.

Through the course of the hearings the New Brunswick situation was mentioned frequently. On the first day, for instance, the Vice-President for Canada of the American Newspaper Guild, Glen Ogilvie, presented a brief which said the Guild was greatly disturbed by the high degree of concentration of ownership of the media, and in support of that commented, "We feel the treatment given news adverse to K.C. Irving's non-newspaper holdings by his New Brunswick papers gives ample demonstration of the potential for dishonesty inherent in such monopoly." (This statement, incidentally, as the brief presented to the Committee by *The Mysterious East* pointed out, was not reported by the Irving press.)

On January 22, the President of the Canadian Labour Congress, Donald MacDonald, testified before the Committee. Asked by Senator McElman whether labour had problems with the media, MacDonald replied, "Well, Senator, I could write a book on my difficulties with the media in Saint John, New Brunswick. I ran a number of strikes there and I was responsible for organization in your province, Senator."

"Yes, I know that is true."

"There is no place in this country," MacDonald went on, "that will stand up by comparison to the experience that we have in Saint John, New Brunswick."

"With the media?"

"With the media."

"Would you," McElman prodded, "care to elaborate on that?"

"I am nearly twenty years removed from what my colleague

refers to as my native habitat, but I can still recall with considerable incense," MacDonald went on vaguely, "as you know, some of my experiences in that city."

"Would you," Senator McElman tried again, "care to elaborate on your experiences with the media?"

"Yes, sure." MacDonald started over. "I will just talk about two experiences. They go far back, because as I say it's nearly twenty years since I have been removed from the Maritimes. I was responsible for two major strikes, the conduct of two major strikes, right in the heart of the city of Saint John. One, the veneer plant that you might recall. . . . "

"I do."

"And the other one with Irving Oil."

"I recall that one as well." McElman, knowing that the details were part of the public record, tried to get MacDonald to push on.

"I was in Saint John, New Brunswick."

"Who," McElman interrupted, making sure to get everything on the record, "were the owners of the veneer plant?"

"Mr. K.C. Irving, as I recall," MacDonald said. "I tried by every means available to get some coverage. There was no TV at that time, and I tried by every means that was possible to get some coverage – these were important strikes at different times, and considerable times apart, I must say – and I never had . . . or never did succeed. As a matter of fact, what I resorted to was printing our own handbills trying to tell factually what was going on, and distributing them free to the pedestrians on the street so we would at least get some dissemination of information in that city."

"You tried both the print media and radio?"

"Both the print media and the radio, that's right."

"Who," McElman asked like a trial lawyer, "owned those, sir?"

"I don't know," MacDonald answered, unwilling to commit himself. "I don't know. But I have my suspicions – but I can't support them."

"Well, I can tell you we have had evidence before the Committee that Mr. K.C. Irving owned them."

"Well, Senator," MacDonald replied, "that was my suspicion." (This exchange, also, went entirely unnoticed in the Irving press. The closest any paper came to mentioning it was in one sentence of a Canadian Press story summarizing the C.L.C. brief printed in the *Telegraph-Journal:* "Trade union news in newspapers is 'skimpy or distorted' ")

But the day on which the whole attention of the Committee was focused on New Brunswick was December 16. On that afternoon the Committee received briefs from K.C. Irving Limited, The Saint John *Telegraph-Journal,* and the Fredericton *Gleaner,* and heard the testimony of Irving himself, Ralph Costello, and Michael Wardell.

Irving's brief was short, direct, and blunt. In it he said that he did not have anything to do with the operation of the media holdings, stated that they had declared no dividends since he had owned them, and made his customary impassioned plea in favour of New Brunswick ownership of New Brunswick endeavours. He concluded: "Almost any New Brunswick corporation, subject to national or international competition, must, if it is to survive successfully, either diversify its activities or itself become national or international in scope. If the latter happens, the head office will no longer remain in the Maritimes. I prefer diversification. Call it conglomerate or what you will – in New Brunswick it contributes to survival." But his opening remarks before the Committee were not so objective. Describing the background of hostility between Wardell and the New Brunswick government of Louis Robichaud, Irving set the keynote of the afternoon – which, with a few breaks for questioning by the senators on the Committee, was to evolve into a concerted attack on Senator McElman. Recounting the way the Robichaud government had revoked Wardell's customary exemption from the provincial prohibition on liquor advertising, referring to McElman's "definite plan", going back several years, to attack his newspaper holdings, and generally impugning the senator's motives, Irving began a verbal attack which was to last the afternoon, and which gave off what

Maclean's magazine would call "the smell of raw power."

Irving's testimony in response to questions was surprisingly frank, and we have quoted extensively from it elsewhere. Two disclosures, however, are important at this point. One involved the Fredericton *Gleaner*. Irving's testimony made it clear that, contrary to Wardell's published remarks, the deal was hardly a simple sale, and that the connections between the *Gleaner* and Irving's empire predated the acquisition that McElman had publicized. Senator J. Harper Prowse began the line of questioning. "Was your most recent acquisition the *Daily Gleaner?* When, on what date, did you acquire the *Gleaner?*"

"What do you mean by 'acquired'?"

"Control . . . complete your arrangements with Brigadier Wardell . . . that you acquired the interests you now have there?" Prowse was clearly confused by Irving's response; what did control mean if not purchase?

Irving was not going to be any help. "I am going to answer your question the only way possible. The date that you are referring to is May 15, 1958, I believe."

"I do not know," Prowse assured him, "what the date is."

"Yes." Irving was not going to volunteer information. "Well, that is when I made a certain arrangement with Brigadier Wardell."

Senator Davey was getting everything down. "May 15?"

"1968." Irving suddenly realized he had misspoken himself earlier. "I am sorry. That is correct; 1968."

Senator Prowse pursued the matter. "When was there any announcement made by anybody as to when that had happened?"

"I am not too sure," Irving said, as well he might. And it was clear he did not want to get into the subject any deeper. "But you understand I might mention this with details . . . certain things are not complete yet with Brigadier Wardell. I do not think that anything . . . that I should go on talking about things that have taken place and . . . possibly not completely dealt with."

Senator Prowse wanted to make sure that Irving did in fact

have control. "Your transaction is not completed? You do not have the full right to exercise the fifty-one per cent or whatever it is you hold now?"

"I have not exercised any voting rights or anything and. . . . " Irving found a way out. "You are asking me to disclose my arrangements with Brigadier Wardell."

"No, sir, I have not."

"All right." Irving was adamant. "Please do not ask me that question."

"What I was asking you," Prowse explained, "was if you are saying that you have not completed your arrangements with him yet."

"We have completed them, yes, to a point, but now I would prefer not to go beyond that unless I am required to. And I am not trying to mislead you, but. . . . "

Davey saw the attempt was fruitless. "We will accept that."

What was interesting about the dialogue was partly that this was the first public indication of the date of Irving's takeover of the *Gleaner*. But perhaps even more significant was Irving's secretiveness and the clear suggestion that the arrangements between University Press and K.C. Irving Limited were complex and probably predated the actual takeover of control.

The other revelation concerned the long-standing attempt by Irving interests to gain control of CKCW in Moncton, the only other television station in the province. Asked whether one of the Irving companies was a minority shareholder in CKCW-TV, Irving replied, "I am not a shareholder of that station."

Senator Prowse clearly had something in mind. "Do you have any interest or any claim on any part of any of the shares of that station that are held by anybody else?"

"Not on the shares; no." Irving was not going to be helpful here either. "You are getting into perhaps a situation there, but I don't own any of the shares."

"Do you exercise any control over any of the shares?"

"No."

Senator Prowse was not going to give up that easily. "Do you have a financial interest in any part of, any interest in the station?"

"Well, no." They didn't have the formula yet. "I have no financial interest in the station."

"As collateral or otherwise?"

"Well, now, that is a different matter." Perhaps he should throw Senator Prowse a hint. "I don't hold any shares as collateral myself."

"Does any one of your companies or your sons?"

"My companies do not hold any shares of collateral," Irving said, continuing the game and throwing another hint, "but there was an obligation of a party that did own those shares. However, I do not hold those shares as collateral."

By this point, everyone was sick of the game. "Thank you." It never became clear that the shares had been owned by Frank Brennan, Irving's first financial partner, with a business association dating from 1929, and that Brennan had sat on the board of directors of CKCW-TV but it did become obvious that there was some connection between CKCW and the Irving empire, and that the acquisition of media outlets was still an active policy of the company.

Ralph Costello was next up. He mounted a vigorous and well-argued defense of the conduct of the newspapers, and an even more vigorous attack on Senator McElman's presence on the Committee, concluding with a demand that McElman withdraw. His testimony centered around issues concerning the operation of the papers, and concluded in a sarcastic debate with McElman about why the newspapers had opposed the Equal Opportunity legislation, with McElman contending that they had opposed it because Irving opposed it, and Costello that they had opposed it because it was bad for the province.

The afternoon ended with Michael Wardell describing his persecution at the hands of the Robichaud government, which, he said, had implemented its plan to destroy him by taking away his liquor advertising revenue and his government printing contracts. It was his contention that the Committee had been set up specifically to harass the *Gleaner,* and he clung to the view in spite of protests by the senators. The Combines Branch "raids", the Davey Committee, the liquor advertising and printing conflicts were all, he contended, part of the same McElman-Robichaud campaign.

Senator McElman, outside the hearing chamber afterward, was quick to point out the diversionary character of the attack on him and the Robichaud government. Calling the afternoon's performance a "circus", he said it seemed to him the Irving people had wasted a lot of their time talking about irrelevant concerns, and that it reminded him of three elephants trying to trample a flea – "They rather got their feet entangled."

The reports of the day's events in the Irving papers were, as might be expected, spectacular; and the angle in their coverage was, equally predictably, to stress the attacks rather than the revelations about Irving's operations. "Irving Charges Robichaud Tried to Destroy Wardell," shrieked a banner headline in the next day's *Gleaner;* "Demands that McElman Resign from Committee Made at Media Inquiry." The previous evening, the *Gleaner* had published a front page story on its own brief, headed "Wardell Says Media Inquiry Part of Attack on Freedom of Press." In both cases the stress was on the roots of McElman's actions in the Robichaud-Irving conflict of the previous decade, and on the persecution of Wardell. "The experiences I have suffered," he said, "in this connection constituted a degree of insult, harassment and attempted intimidation never before, I believe, applied to the free press of any country under a democratic government."

The *Telegraph-Journal* also stressed the attack on McElman, though not quite to Wardell's hysterical extent. Its front page the morning after the Irving testimony featured a four-column box the length of the front page, topped by a picture of Irving glowering at Davey, and headed "McElman Challenged at Press Hearing – Irving Says Premier Tried to Ruin Wardell."

Another burst of publicity attended the tabling of the first volume of the Davey Committee's report, *The Uncertain Mirror,* the following December 9. For while the report did not focus on the situation in New Brunswick, it did make its opinion clear. And it did so in what were often memorable terms. It said, for instance, that "New Brunswick, of course, is the outstanding example of conglomerate ownership." and called the situation "about as flagrant an example of abusing the public interest as you're likely to find in Canada," claiming that it had produced in the Maritimes what could only be described as a "journalistic disaster area." It was vivid in its description of the kind of bad journalism that characterized such an area. "There is a third kind of newspaper in Canada," the report said, " – the kind that prints news releases intact, that seldom extends its journalistic enterprise beyond coverage of the local trout festival, that hasn't annoyed anyone important in years. Their city rooms are refuges for the frustrated and disillusioned, and their editorial pages a daily testimony to the notion that Chamber-of-Commerce boosterism is an adequate substitute for community service. It is our sad impression that a great many, if not most Canadian newspapers fall into this classification. Interestingly enough, among them are some of the most profitable newspapers in the country. A number of these newspapers are owned by K.C. Irving."

The committee also took some pains to make clear the kind of complex relationship that might obtain between owners of newspapers and the papers' policies. Concentration of ownership such as was found in New Brunswick, they said, "could also – but not necessarily – lead to a situation where the news (which we must start thinking of as a public resource, like electricity) is controlled and manipulated by a small group of individuals and corporations whose view of What's Fit to Print may closely coincide with What's Good for General Motors, or What's Good for Business, or What's Good for My Friends Down at the Club. There is some evidence, in fact, which suggests that we are in that boat already."

The publicity generated by the report was spectacular and,

on the part of the Maritime press, coverage was almost uniformly hostile. Front-page editorials in the Irving papers attacked it as biased, inaccurate, possessed of "sickening weaknesses" and an affront to public credibility. But for the long run, the report had brought up issues which were not likely to be disposed of by vilification of the Committee's motives and membership. The extent of Irving's domination of New Brunswick, for instance, had never before been made so clear to so many people. The subtlety of the relation between ownership and editorial policy had never received such intense public scrutiny. Opinion ranged from the report's suggestion of the "What's Good for My Friends Down at the Club" hypothesis to Senator McElman's darker suspicions. "It is not," he said in a Senate speech the spring following the report's publication, "primarily the balance sheet that concerns these financial-industrial tycoons. . . . It is not the prestige of being owners and publishers of newspapers. It is not the earnest desire to lead, editorially, public thought toward progressive social reform and higher human purpose. The primary purpose is none of these. The primary purpose is to grasp power and more power. They want the power to choose and appoint publishers and editors who share their philosophy, or who will at least operate the newspapers in strict accordance with their philosophy."

By hiring "pawns", McElman charged, the owner puts himself in a position in which he never has to actually exercise his power. "His choice of top pawn or pawns ensures that things will work to his entire satisfaction. He can then testify publicly, or even before committees of Parliament, that he has never interfered with the operation or editorial policies of his newspapers. He can even appear mystified to explain, under questioning, just why he ever bothered to buy up newspapers. He really cannot explain why he is in the business."

"There," he concluded, "is the power, the power to decide what will and what will not become public issues. The greatest concern lies in the power to determine what will not become public issues."

It seems clear that, in the Irving case at least, the answer lies somewhere between those two viewpoints. But whatever one chose to believe about the question, it was clear that for once it was someone other than newspaper owners who were deciding what was to be a public issue – that regardless of the preferences of the owners, the question of press ownership had become a major public concern.

Equally public was a new level of understanding of press monopoly in general and Irving's in particular. In general terms, the Davey Committee made the public aware of the immense profitability of mediocre newspapers, and the reasons why it was desirable to reinvest the profits – in equipment and in other newspapers – rather than to declare dividends. "Under our tax laws, shareholders are taxed only on the earnings they receive as dividends. The remainder, the profits the company keeps in the treasury as retained earnings, aren't taxable until they're distributed. The effect is that corporations which keep earning profits build up larger and larger reserves of retained earnings." These, in turn, drive the price of shares up, allowing shareholders to take the profit in nontaxable capital gains rather than in taxable dividends. And of course the retained earnings must be reinvested somehow and there is only so much machinery a newspaper can absorb. Beyond that, what better investment for a newspaper company than another newspaper? Additionally, of course, largeness is itself an advantage because the larger you are the easier it is to borrow money or (if you aren't Irving) raise equity capital by selling shares to the public.

An implication of the Senate investigation which is more specifically applicable to the Irving media empire is the documentation of the fact that the empire was more than a mere accident. It was through the Committee's transcripts that New Brunswickers first had an opportunity to learn the dates and extent of Irving's ownership of the media, of his attempts to gain control of CKCW-TV in Moncton, and of his company's application for the cable television franchise for Saint John in 1968 – an application, by Irving's Saint John Cablevision, whose aim was, as Costello himself testified before the Davey

Committee, to preclude someone else getting the franchise. This pattern of activity makes it clear that the dinosaur had – and has – as a policy the aggressive acquisition of a media monopoly. It had been known for years in New Brunswick that Irving would buy anything – anything at all – in the lumber business (at a price); now it was clear that the same applied to the media.

There is an important consideration, however, which the Davey report – along with most commentators – have missed, although the basis for perceiving it was laid in the report. That consideration can be phrased like this: in measuring the power of a newspaper, its effect on public opinion, the public editorial position taken by the paper is dwarfed in importance by the paper's unspoken, and probably unacknowledged, assumptions. This can be made clearer by a couple of examples.

In 1965 the Saint John Common Council proposed to build a bridge across the harbour. The bridge was an important project, and during the year there were infrequent reports in the paper of plans, of construction contracts to be let, and so forth. In October, however, K.C. Irving suddenly decided that the bridge would be bad for Saint John (as well as for his fleets of trucks and buses, which would have to pay tolls) and that a bypass (which would be cheaper and thus toll-free) would be a better plan. For a month, the papers were full of reports of the "citizen's committee" that was formed by an Irving legal adviser and one of Irving's sons, and suddenly the papers' editorial policies were unanimously in favour of the bypass, as was the radio station. Whether the papers were, as McElman charged during the hearings, co-ordinated by the Irving interests, or, on the other hand, as Costello claimed, simply convinced by the logic of the "citizen's committee's" presentation, the effect was the same. Brigadier Wardell wrote an editorial on October 14, offering congratulations on the "extraordinary barrage of publicity used by Mr. K.C. Irving and those who support him in Saint John, to bring about a lastditch revision of the harbour bridge scheme, which must be startling to those not conversant with the use of all media of public information to create the impact of an idea."

Interestingly, however, the effort failed utterly and, perhaps surprisingly, the Common Council unanimously voted, after studying Irving's counterproposal, to proceed with the bridge. The publicity blitz – perhaps precisely because it was a blitz, and everyone recognized it as such – failed.

At the same time that Senator McElman asked Costello about the bridge campaign, however, he brought up another issue whose implications are quite different, perhaps opposite. "Was there not," he asked, "co-ordination of the media in announcing the expansion of the Brunswick Mining and Smelting project in October of 1964?" "No," answered Costello, "not co-ordination." Certainly there had been a major event, and the papers had all covered it. But co-ordination? Certainly not. Later that afternoon, McElman came back in with a copy of the front page of the October 27, 1964 *Telegraph-Journal* and described it at some length. To say the least, it was an eye-catching story: a province-wide television announcement by Louis Robichaud and John D. Park, at that time Irving's right-hand man, had announced a $117,000,000 expansion at Brunswick. This formed the substance of a red banner across the top, in a "circus" make-up; the black headline below the paper's name said "Steel Mill to Cost $64 Million." A smaller headline below that said "$90 Million Benefit to New Brunswick." A two-column, ten-inch box was headed "What it Will Mean to N.B." and included a boldface list of consequences. About seventy-five per cent of the front page, an equal amount of page three, and a two-column, fifteen-inch editorial were taken up with the announcement. There were elaborate maps and diagrams and the complete text of Robichaud's announcement; there were photos of Robichaud and Park standing before charts. (There was not, however, any mention of the fact that Engineering Consultants Limited, the company headed by Park which was planning the expansion, was a wholly-owned subsidiary of K.C. Irving Limited.)

Concluding his description, McElman then explained that the elaborate detail was not the result of eager and aggressive newsgathering, but rather the result of a meeting between personnel of Engineering Consultants and the papers and the television station, at which E.C.L. had laid out the whole campaign. After some controversy about whether Costello himself had been at that meeting (McElman claimed to remember him; Costello claimed not to remember such a meeting), McElman asked, "Would you find it surprising if I recalled that on this occasion representatives of the broadcast media and of the newspapers did take part in the preparation of this whole production in advance . . . ? Would you be surprised if I recalled that, let's say, senior representatives of both broadcast and the print media were brought in to discuss this and the whole thing was laid out, the charts were prepared with the assistance of art staffs so they would show up well on TV and this sort of thing, as well as reproductions in newspapers, and that the whole effort was co-ordinated well in advance?"

Costello was cautious. "The question which you asked me was would it surprise me if this sort of thing did take place, and the answer is, no, it would not surprise me. It could take place at any time. If a press conference was called – "

McElman interrupted, saying it had been no press conference. Costello said that whatever it was, it wouldn't surprise him on a thing of that size. McElman asked George Cromwell, the general manager of New Brunswick Broadcasting, whether he didn't recall the meeting, and then turned to W.A. Stewart, the station manager.

"Yes, I recall some preparation. There were preparations made for paid broadcasts and we were asked to arrange a network of stations, if I remember correctly, which we did. I produced a program and the only other thing that I know, that I recall, was that there was great secrecy about it. The talk was put on a TelePrompTer I believe, and that was delivered to me a matter of an hour or less before the program went on the air to safeguard against a premature break on the thing. The program, I think, went on the air somewhere between 6.30 and 7.00 and I produced it."

A few moments later, McElman restated his point. "The

point of the whole exercise is that I do recall it very clearly that there was co-ordination. There was no press conference as such. There was a co-ordination. The co-ordination was done, not at the insistence of government, but at the insistence of E.C.L., a wholly-owned subsidiary, under the direction of Mr. John Park."

Costello was admitting nothing. "Well," he said, "that is information that you have and I am not familiar with it." But he didn't have to admit anything. McElman's point was made. Its implications, however, were not yet clear. For though both these incidents do show that the Irving dinosaur is capable of co-ordinating the media to its own advantage, there is a fundamental difference between them. In the bridge controversy the clear intention of the papers was persuasive, and as such their editorial position was of central importance. In the case of the Brunswick expansion, however, no one realized that the intent was equally persuasive; it seems clear from Stewart's testimony and Costello's that they thought of the announcement as purely informational. The decisions about the value of the project, and the value of announcing it in a spectacular way, seem to have been taken long before the problem became a conscious one. No one raised a question as to whether a mere projection by an almost unknown and as yet untried company was worth such an overwhelming propaganda burst. If someone had pointed out that much of the projected new industry was very hypothetical at best, and might not develop (as indeed it has not), he would, clearly, not have been taken seriously. So the effect of the announcement – and the even more spectacular announcement the following spring of the opening of the first phase (which involved not only equally elaborate coverage, but a special twelve-page "mining section" of the paper) was, in fact, as persuasive in intent as the campaign to relocate the bridge had been. The difference was that in the Brunswick case no one acknowledged it, and there was no test of its effectiveness. But clearly its effect was to make people take John Park's and Kenneth Irving's pipe dreams with solemn seriousness, and to build into

the popular consciousness an assumption about the importance of such industrial announcements and such plans. That
such things work brilliantly can be made clear by reading the
letters columns of the papers every time Irving's name comes
up or every time someone questions New Brunswick's blind
commitment to the sponsoring of resource-based industry.

If the Davey Committee failed to stress adequately the
force of such unspoken assumptions in the conduct of the
press, and too often projected a paper's opinion and measured
its impact from its editorial columns, it did not miss an equally
crucial point, which is that for the average citizen there is little
recourse when he is unhappy with the press. A common argument of the newspaper publishers was that "the public is our
judge" – indeed, that argument was central to Ralph Costello's
defense of the Irving monopoly. The Davey Committee, in its
report, quoted Donald Cameron's testimony: "In Fredericton,
a good many of us have looked at our daily newspaper, affec-
tionately nicknamed *The Daily Weiner,* and we have judged.
We consider the *Gleaner* a dreadful newspaper. So what? No
consequences follow from that judgement. There isn't any
provision for any consequences to follow. This committee is
the first opportunity I can recall for any dissatisfied citizen to
do anything meaningful at all about the media."

For some aspects of the problem, however, there is recourse, as Maritimers were reminded in the spring following
the media report's appearance. On March 31 and April 1 and
2, investigators from the Combines Branch again conducted a
search of executive files in the New Brunswick newspaper
offices, under a warrant signed by Judge Charles F. Tweeddale
of Burton, in whose court the preliminary hearing was to be
held. Again there were anguished cries from the newspapers
concerned; and on the 27th of April a hearing was held in Saint
John in the court of Mr. Justice Albany M. Robichaud of the
New Brunswick Supreme Court on whether the warrants
should not be quashed and the evidence seized by the investigators returned. The warrants were not quashed, however,
and on December 8 charges were laid at Judge Tweeddale's

court in Burton. There were four charges. The first applied to K.C. Irving Limited, and asserted that the corporation was party to a merger in which it took over University Press, whereby "competition in the producing, supplying, selling or dealing in English language newspapers in New Brunswick" was lessened. The second charged that K.C. Irving Limited, Moncton Publishing, and University Press were parties to the formation of a combine; this applied to the dates between 1948 and 1960, when the law had been changed, and a third charge covered the period between 1960 and the present, under the new law. A fourth charge stated that the four companies had formed a monopoly. In the first cases, Irving, Costello and Wardell were declared to be parties to the offence, though they were not charged.

Preliminary hearings – to determine whether the evidence was sufficient to bring the companies to trial – were held in Judge Tweeddale's court some ten miles below Fredericton on the banks of the St. John River during the spring, and on July 17, Judge Tweeddale decided that there was indeed enough evidence to try the companies.

But the legal problem was a complex one. Canada's anti-combines laws, as D.H.W. Henry had testified before the Davey Committee, were "too blunt an instrument to deal with concentration in its incipiency and are probably too inflexible to deal effectively with the real issues involved in continuing concentration in mass media."

There are a number of reasons for this. One explains why the broadcasting companies were not to be involved in the trial. The Combines Investigation Act only applies where there is a product. In the case of a newspaper, the daily stack of paper itself is a product – but, clearly, there is no tangible product from a broadcasting station and so the law simply does not apply. But even where the law does apply, it is hardly a model of clarity. There are, for instance, two tests for whether a merger is unlawful under the present anti-combines legislation: it must restrain or limit competition, and the limitation must be detrimental to the public. But it has never been made clear precisely what the "detriment of the public" amounts to – and this question, in the case of newspapers, is clearly a crucial one. For if, as courts have normally held, "detriment" must be measured in financial terms, the case is next to impossible to prove. Even if it were to be allowed that the detriment of the public could be interpreted more broadly, it is pretty difficult to demonstrate that the public's ignorance of the whole history of the *Irving Whale* before its sinking is "detrimental".

Equally interesting – and equally disheartening – is the fact that Combines Act investigations and prosecutions have never produced a divesting order, an order to break up the monopoly. There have been only two important precedents in the courts. One involved a series of mergers which allowed Canadian Breweries to dominate the brewing market, and another which involved a British Columbia sugar refinery acquiring a Manitoba one and creating a monopoly of sugar refining in western Canada. But neither of these eventuated in a divesting order. The brewing case was dismissed on the grounds that, first, since the price of beer was regulated in any case, the Combines legislation didn't apply, and, second, the degree of concentration – between sixty-five and seventy per cent of the market – was not sufficient to consitute a violation. The sugar case was struck down because there still was competition from eastern Canada. And that's all the precedents there were – hardly an encouraging prospect.

D.H.W. Henry said, in his presentation to the Davey Committee, that the courts "have held that competition must be virtually stiffled before the merger can be struck down under the law," and that the courts "have been reluctant to enter into any sophisticated economic analysis of the situation resulting from the merger and have tended in lieu thereof to find a reasonable doubt in the face of evidence of some competition remaining."

Which brings us to another fatal flaw in the Combines legislation; it is written as part of the Criminal Code, which means that the case must be established "beyond a reasonable doubt" – an almost impossible task in economic situations.

Another implication of the fact that it's a criminal procedure is that there can be no regulations based on it – either the action is illegal or not, and the only test is the court. Moreover, there's no way (because the regulations do not exist) to proceed against a monopoly in its early stages.

As Henry pointed out, the law "could be invoked only in the final stages of monopolization when concentration has proceeded far beyond the degree where competition remains in effective force."

Even before Judge Tweeddale decided the case was a substantial one, however, two things happened which made it almost an academic matter. On December 23, 1971, K.C. Irving himself had relinquished all his personal property in Canada to the corporation, turned over effective control of his business affairs to his sons, and left New Brunswick to take up residence in Bermuda, thus effectively removing the central figure from the stage.

And then, on the following June 16, it was announced that the media empire had been reorganized. K.C. Irving Limited, which had owned the Moncton, Fredericton and Saint John publishing companies outright, had transferred its interest in Fredericton's University Press Limited (publisher of the *Daily Gleaner*) and in Moncton Publishing (the *Times and Transcript*) to the youngest Irving brother, John, who had in turn given up all his interest in K.C. Irving Limited, the family's central holding company. In addition, K.C. Irving Limited relinquished its control of New Brunswick Publishing (the *Telegraph-Journal* and the *Evening Times-Globe*), with James Irving (the oldest) and Arthur Irving each acquiring a forty per cent interest in the company. K.C. Irving Limited retained only a twenty per cent share.

Whether this was done in order to forestall a feared divesting order, or as part of a more general dividing up of the whole dinosaur, was not clear. But as many New Brunswickers knew, whatever the formal arrangements might be, blood is thicker than paper. The media empire remained intact. Even so, something fundamental had changed in New Brunswick; control of the province's access to information could never again be restored to the level of completeness that Irving had attained in the fifties and sixties.

The question remained, however, whether New Brunswick's history might not have been vastly different if the media had been aggressively independent, sceptical and tough-minded during the period of Irving's expansion. Would the Brunswick fiasco have occurred if journalists had been more sceptical about all those grandiosely optimistic announcements? Would Irving companies have been able to acquire and retain all the lavish tax concessions and legal exemptions which underwrote their spectacular successes? How far might Equal Opportunity have changed the face of the province if the money to finance it could have been squeezed from the corporations? Would pulp mills, oil refineries, and deepwater ports in other hands, forced to compete with each other, have benefited the province more than Irving's stupendous single-handed effort?

Almost equally important, would the rest of Canada have seen a different New Brunswick, one, perhaps, posing different problems and requiring different policies, if the image of the province presented in the national press had not been composed at Canadian Press desks in Irving city rooms? Probably even more important is the fact that the major sources for a history of New Brunswick in the twentieth century are to be found in the newspapers' files – and what is included there is what the Irving press found important enough to cover and significant enough to preserve. How different might future histories of that province be if the newspapers had been owned by Atlantic Sugar? Or by completely independent professional journalists?

Such questions can probably never be answered definitely. But if you accept that the dinosaur has been the most important single element in the history of New Brunswick in the middle of this century, there can't be much doubt that New Brunswick – and eastern Canada as a whole – would be a vastly different place if the dinosaur had never existed. Nor can it be seriously disputed that the dinosaur's control of the media – whether directly through ownership or indirectly through influences – has been central to its control of the province and therefore to its own growth.

As to the future, it is clear that the dinosaur's growth will be slowed, at least – perhaps arrested – by the departure of its guiding genius from the affairs of at least the New Brunswick section of what had become by the onset of the seventies a multi-national empire. As the dinosaur's vigour slackens, the importance of its domination of the media will decrease. But its imprint on New Brunswick's history and the shape of its society will not fade.

Dinosaurs and Monuments

Any historian will tell you that few eras end or begin on specific or identifiable dates. In this respect – as in so many others – New Brunswick's history is hardly unique. For instance, the date on which the most important era in its history ended is shrouded in mystery and confusion. Sometime before the end of the year 1971, the driving force behind the mushrooming expansion of the Irving empire was suddenly removed, as K.C. Irving officially left the province to take up residence outside Canada. Characteristically, the move was accomplished in almost total silence, and it wasn't until almost three weeks into the new year – on the 18th of January – that it was officially announced that K.C. Irving was no longer residing in New Brunswick.

Equally characteristic was the announcement itself, which wasn't a prepared statement, but a response to a phone call from the staff of the *Telegraph-Journal* in Saint John. The reporters were reacting to a flurry of rumours concerning Irving – a flurry that began when he suddenly cancelled a speaking engagement in Saint John, and when it became known that his home phone number – previously listed in the Saint John telephone directory, and usually answered by Irving himself – had been changed to an unlisted number. The level of secrecy maintained about the move is perhaps clearest when you consider that the *Telegraph-Journal* staff could only find out that Irving was in Nassau after what they described as a "day-long series of checks." The paper is, after all, an Irving company, and its publisher, Ralph Costello, is a close associate of Irving.

Irving's treatment of the press's questions, too, was consistent with his normal practice. Asked whether he had left in order to avoid new taxation rules coming into effect in 1972, he replied that rather than answer the question, he would make a brief statement. That statement was, if nothing else, indeed brief. "I am no longer residing in New Brunswick. My sons, J.D. Irving, A.L. Irving, and J.E. Irving, are carrying on the various businesses. As far as anything else goes, I do not choose to discuss the matter further." That was it. He declined to say whether Nassau was his new permanent residence (it was not; within a few months he was a permanent resident of Bermuda). But he did answer one further question: asked how long ago he had left the province, he said, "I left last year."

That "last year", the *Telegraph-Journal* inferred, was a reference to the new estate tax situation. The federal government had announced that it was abolishing such taxes; and various provinces – including the four Atlantic Provinces – had announced that they would take over the collection of estate taxes, and that their laws, even though they could not be passed until later in the year, would be retroactive to January 1, 1972, the date on which the federal taxes had lapsed. The paper suggested that the clear implication of Irving's statement was that he had left to avoid such taxes.

Beyond that, the rest was silence: whether Irving had actually left because of the tax situation, or whether he was retiring from active business and leaving affairs to his sons, was left for the world to figure out. So was the official date of Irving's departure, which seems, from a business point of view, to have been December 23, 1971. At least, that is the date on which all of Irving's private property in New Brunswick (his home, for instance, and any land held in his or his wife's name) was turned over to the corporation. But when Irving physically left the province was as impenetrable a question as his motives and his intentions.

Politicians, the business community, and the press were – predictably – among the first to react to the announcement. But their reactions were not what one might have predicted. Premier Hatfield, in a difficult position because it was his government which was introducing the provincial estate taxes which many people thought responsible for Irving's departure, could only say that "his decision to take up residence outside the province is regretted." Others were more forceful. New Brunswick's Liberal opposition leader, Robert Higgins, who was less constrained, called it "a severe blow to the province" and took out after the government for announcing that it was going to take over the estate tax from Ottawa.

The business community was equally concerned. John G. McD. Brown, president of the Saint John Board of Trade, said, "I think it is a tragic loss – not only to New Brunswick, but to Canada." But most were concerned with Irving's motives; the Sobey family, it seemed, were even considering leaving "the home stores" to shift for themselves while they left the country to avoid the new taxes. The president of Halifax Developments Limited (owners of Scotia Square in downtown Halifax) said that Irving's departure showed that the tax laws were making it impossible for industrialists to stay in the Maritimes – or, for that matter, in Canada.

But what was surprising was the generally lukewarm attitude of the press toward Irving's departure. Whether this was because, even though the press felt generally that the taxes were a bad thing, they hesitated to praise Irving's departure – an act which, if not exactly unpatriotic, was certainly at odds with his declared love of his home province – was not clear. But most newspapers contented themselves with commenting – if they commented at all – on the unfortunate side effects of the taking up of the estate tax by the provinces. The Moncton *Times* for instance, pointed out that while Irving's departure was "a great loss", its major concern was the apprehension that Irving's leaving might be the first of a series of departures by large-scale capitalists.

The only paper to play the old tune was the *Telegraph-Journal,* which marked the occasion by cranking up a heart-rending editorial. "Kenneth Colin Irving, the Buctouche boy who loved New Brunswick so much that he stayed at home to seek and make his fortune, has left his native province," it began. "Yet, despite the explicit nature of his brief statement," it said a few paragraphs later, "there are those who cannot bring themselves to believe he is no longer at his office in the Golden Ball Building on Union Street in the heart of Saint John, personally directing his vast enterprises by telephone, private radio and direct verbal communication with key executives who touch every fibre of the province's business and industrial activity."

Calling him "a man obsessed with New Brunswick", and "a man in love with New Brunswick", pointing out that he has "truly accomplished the impossible, not once but many times", and listing in passing some of his achievements, the editorial moved into the series of rhetorical questions which was its climax:

> "But is he a man apart? Is he one of a kind? Is he one of the last of the great twentieth century giants of Canadian industry?
>
> "Is New Brunswick richer or poorer, not in a financial sense but in every other way, because he has taken leave? Is New Brunswick richer or poorer? Does the sun shine? Is there water in the ocean? Is it dark at night?"

But aside from this elegy from the flagship of the Irving media empire (and the weekly King's County *Record*'s comment that Irving's departure was "the darkest day in the history of the province"), the reaction of the press generally was cool. Many papers didn't comment editorially at all. The Canadian section of *Time* magazine – long a close observer of Irving, presumably on the grounds that he's as close as Canada comes to a Howard Hughes – didn't even mention that Irving had left.

Equally important, especially in a place like New Brunswick where letters to the editor are a central forum for the expression of public opinion, was the fact that there were virtually no letters to the editors mourning Irving's departure. In the two weeks following the announcement, there was one letter in the Fredericton *Daily Gleaner* expressing regret, which was balanced by one assailing Irving's hypocrisy, in the *Telegraph-Journal*. And that was all. The magic was clearly gone. For whatever reasons, Irving had ceased to be the darling of writers of letters to the editor, as well as of the writers of editorials. Whether this was caused by his "unpatriotic" departure or by more long-term considerations was doubtful. Certainly it seems to have been the general opinion that Irving had not been forced out of the province by the government's actions. As the *Gleaner* pointed out, Irving "would still have had to pay estate taxes had Ottawa stayed on its former course, and, if estate taxes were the reason for his going, he would probably have left anyhow." The clear implication was that however much a K.C. Irving might be, personally, "a man obssessed with New Brunswick", "a man in love with New Brunswick", when it came to the financial crunch he would go to Bermuda. K.C. Irving's romance with New Brunswick seemed finally to be over, by mutual consent.

But the question about Irving's motives remained baffling. Had he, in fact, left to avoid inheritance duties, as the *Telegraph-Journal* had inferred? Irving himself had made no such statement. And his departure would hardly make him unlikely to escape the taxes, since the new laws would tax the beneficiaries according to their residence – that is, if Irvings' sons resided in New Brunswick at the time of his death, they would be taxed in New Brunswick, regardless of their father's residence.

No, the situation is far more complex than would be indicated by those who argue that he left to avoid succession duties. In part, by leaving before December 31, Irving was able to act under the old federal estate tax law, which has a number of loopholes that were to be plugged by the new provincial legislation. Under the old law, if the deceased established foreign residence and if all the property was held outside Canada at the time of death – in a holding company, for instance, like those already established in Nassau by Irving – then no taxes could be collected whether or not the beneficiaries lived in Canada. The question of whether the new laws will apply to Irving's case will likely be a knotty one, and perhaps Irving feels that his heirs would be likely to win it.

Another possibility is that under the new income tax law, you must pay tax on accrued capital gains before you leave the country. But since the tax will only be payable on gains accruing after January 1, 1972, there seems to have been no rush for Irving to leave so quickly – unless he was merely unwilling to go through the major task of evaluating his assets at the beginning of the new system.

In the absence of a statement of his own motives – and if past experience is any guide, we are not going to get an explanation from Irving – one can only guess as to his motives. One virtual certainty is that they are not simple; another is that they transcend the merely financial. It is not impossible that Irving saw his departure as part of a campaign against the increasing taxation of capital in Canada: the combination of the new capital-gains tax with the continuation of succession duties and gift taxes represents a trend in government which can hardly have pleased him. And there is no doubt that his most-used weapon in relations with government has traditionally been the threat to pull out.

Another hypothesis that has not been taken very seriously is the possibility that Irving is doing what his only official statement claimed he was doing – retiring from active business in New Brunswick. And certainly it would not be unlike him to combine such a personal motive with the more public ones, such as complicating his affairs in order to increase the chances of circumventing the estate taxes, or putting pressure on the government of New Brunswick to allow estate taxes to lapse.

Whatever the truth – and it is not at all unlikely that it will never be known – the mystery itself is as characteristic of Irving's business career as anything could be. That even his motives for bowing out should be doubtful is entirely typical of K.C. Irving – this apparently uncomplicated New Brunswicker who so thoroughly defies comprehension.

Predicting the effects of his departure on the province which has been at once the beneficiary and the victim of his astonishing economic accomplishments is almost as difficult as understanding his motives. One clear result, however, is that the vital spark which made the dinosaur so remarkably dynamic will be gone. In any census of the qualities which make Irving's businesses different from others, it becomes clear that an astonishingly large proportion of those qualities – the combativeness, the tenacity, the tendency toward the concrete and the physical rather than the abstract – are closely connected with the personality of K.C. Irving himself. And such qualities are not normally inherited, nor is the simple creative energy which never seemed to allow Irving to rest, to merely maintain. With those qualities gone – or at least not present in anything like the quantities which Irving supplied – and with the leadership of the corporation divided among his three sons and their advisers, it seems likely that the dinosaur will become increasingly quiet and senescent, that even if it continues to grow (growth is, after all, a condition of life in the business world) its growth will not be so all-consuming as it has been in the past. The dinosaur will, in other words, stop being a dinosaur and become a monument.

And like any appropriate monument, its size and shape will reflect the stature of its subject. The casual passerby will be moved to stop and muse for a moment on the giants of days gone by. But he will not be threatened – except, perhaps, by ghosts of the past in his own mind – or excited by the monument as he might have been by what it stands for. And as the monster petrifies and its outlines become clearer, like dinosaur bones imprinted in the rocks of another age, our astonishment that such things could have once been will rival that of the discoverers of earlier dinosaur bones, earlier relics of an antediluvian age of giants.